FRANCHISING
FOR FREE

FRANCHISING FOR FREE

Owning Your Own Business Without Investing Your Own Cash

Dennis L. Foster

John Wiley & Sons, Inc.
New York • Chichester • Brisbane • Toronto • Singapore

Publisher: Stephen Kippur
Editor: David Sobel
Managing Editor: Andrew Hoffer
Editing, Design & Production: Publications Development Company

Library of Congress Cataloging-in-Publication Data

Foster, Dennis L.
  Franchising for free.

    1. Franchises (Retail trade)—United States.
I. Title.
HF5429.235.U5F67   1987   658.8'708   87-13379
ISBN 0-471-62554-X
ISBN 0-471-62555-8 (pbk.)

Printed in the United States of America

  10 9 8 7 6 5 4

Contents

Preface

The figures on franchising are impressive: more than 2,000 chains generating some $556 billion in annual sales. Franchisors and their advocates like to point out that eighty percent of all businesses eventually fail, most in the first year, whereas of all franchise outlets only slightly more than one and a half percent fail each year.

It is a small wonder that, in today's atmosphere of intense competition and corporate takeovers, interest in franchising is at an all time high. The reason is obvious: judging from the facts, a franchise offers the average person a viable route to the American Dream of business ownership and independence. People enter franchising in an attempt to avoid the usual risks and pitfalls associated with starting a new business. They believe they are purchasing a tried-and-true business concept backed by the know-how and services of an experienced franchisor.

But no matter what anyone predicts, investing in a franchise can be a risky proposition. Remember that the number one reason any business fails is inadequate financing. The second pitfall is bad management, which often translates into poor planning. This book was written specifically to address these two crucial issues of a franchise decision.

Why a book on franchise financing and planning, if franchising has built-in safeguards against failure? According to the Department of Commerce, last year there were a record number of failures in the franchise field, with 78 franchisors responsible for 5,667 outlets going out of business. That number may seem small in relation to the total field of almost half a million outlets, but it does not consider franchise owners who continue to operate at a loss or by barely breaking even. Nor does it include owners who discover midway through their contract terms that the business falls short of the franchise salesman's promises. There are no hard statistics on the number or percentage of these marginal outlets, but to be sure, they do exist.

In short, though a franchise may reduce many of the risks and pitfalls of starting a business, it does not preclude the need for adequate financing and sound, basic business planning. Unfortunately, very few franchisors will help you with a business plan until after you have signed a contract and paid the franchisee fee. (Some not even then.) Yet, the time when a business plan is most needed is before the contract is signed.

There are many aspects to evaluating a franchise opportunity, but none is more important than evaluating its financial outlook. A franchisor's statement of projected earnings is not a reliable estimate of what you can realistically expect to earn in the business. Only a good financial plan can provide an accurate depiction of your financial future in a franchise. It can also help you obtain financing from an investor, lender, or venture capitalist. Fundamentally, it can help you decide whether a particular franchise opportunity is right for you.

So, though *Franchising For Free* focuses on how to finance a franchise, it is also an indispensable guide to planning and setting up the business. To our knowledge, no other book explores these topics in as much depth and detail. Yet no two areas will be more crucial to making the right decision about a franchise investment and, ultimately, in determining your success or failure in the business.

Introduction

In today's aggressive economic atmosphere, it is tempting to divide American business into two adversary universes, one composed of big corporations, the other of small-time, independent operators. Consider this alarming statistic: 80 percent of all businesses that will be started this year are already destined to fail.

Franchising shatters that mold. In the franchise relationship, big business and small-time operators discard their century-old acrimony and join for mutual benefit in a sturdy bed of conjugal bliss. This wedding of commercial interests actually creates an interdependence between the big corporation and the small business owner. It encourages and sustains entrepreneurs, rather than threatening them, and forms a mutual-success scenario in which both parties must grow together to survive.

THE FRANCHISE FORMULA

Franchises account for over a third of all retail trade in the United States. Half a million Americans own and operate

1

franchise outlets, employing more than four million members of the work force. The Commerce Department feels so positively about this powerful economic force that it calls franchising the last avenue to the American Dream of independence, business ownership, and self-management.

Franchisors often refer to their systems as "cookie-cutters," stamping out near-clones of their original, prototype businesses. As a result, a franchise establishment wraps the consumer in a security blanket of sameness. Consider, as an example, a Howard Johnson's or Holiday Inn. No matter where the hotel is located or who actually owns it, you are assured of roughly the same service, price, cleanliness, and decor.

Likewise, you expect New Coke® to taste the same in Old England or New Mexico. From togs to tacos, from computers to cars, the most popular stores—and the most popular products—are the ones that cater to the common denominator in public taste. Franchises, for their uniform operating standards and cookie-cutter designs, are the very paradigm of that common denominator.

You do sacrifice some measure of independence as a franchisee. You also sacrifice a percentage of the take—a royalty on all gross revenues. On the opposite side of the coin, the average franchise owner earns twenty percent more than other small business owners. Most important of all, a franchise is four and half times more likely to succeed than any other form of business.

FINANCING THE FRANCHISE

Assume, then, that you are one of the hundred thousand or so Americans who will set out this year to start their own businesses. Let us also assume you want to be among the twenty percent who will survive and have decided franchising is your best-odds route to self-management and independence. Third, let's assume there is one minor hitch: you don't have the cash.

Despair not. In this book, you will discover *five* ways to get into a franchise business without a cash investment:

1. by obtaining seed capital from a SBIC
2. by qualifying for assistance from a MESBIC
3. by securing an SBA-guaranteed loan
4. by attracting a venture capital group or independent investor on the prowl for new small-business startups
5. by leveraging a franchisor

Franchising For Free is divided into three sections. The first section describes detailed techniques for packaging a Business Financial Plan for a franchise start-up. The content covers how to analyze the market, forecast revenue and expenses, prepare a management plan, and determine the payout to investors. Case histories and examples accompany a step-by-step blueprint for creating a venture proposal.

The second section offers concrete tips for determining the best source for financing, soliciting financial assistance, and submitting your proposal. You will find names, addresses, and phone numbers to help you locate investment companies, financial assistance agencies, and venture capital groups.

The third section discusses both why and how franchisors often finance their franchisees' initial investments. The book concludes with a directory of more than 250 major franchisors who offer financial assistance, with their names, addresses, and phone numbers.

Of course, nothing of value is completely free. In this book's title, "free" means more than leveraging a franchise investment. It stands for the independence, self-management, and self-esteem that set a successful small business owner apart from the crowd. Indeed, the primary reason for investing in franchises is the desire to be one's own boss. So this book is not just about franchising for free, but franchising for personal and financial freedom.

SECTION

1

Entering the World of Franchising

1

The Franchise

George liked to tell a variation of an old joke: How many bosses does it take to change a light bulb? The answer, according to George, is nine: one to conduct a feasibility analysis, one to file a staff requirements report, one to approve the purchase of the light bulb, and five to supervise.

Granted, it's not very funny if you happen to be a boss, but in George's case it was symptomatic of a deep, inner yearning.

Not that George failed to get along with his boss. "You can always tell the ones who get along with the boss," he used to say every year at the office Christmas party. "They're the ones with shoe polish on their lips." Even the boss laughed.

George had worked in the same field a dozen years, and for the same company, the last seven. He rose early, commuted to work as the sun was just peeking over the telephone wires, and never failed to clock in by 8:30. George dressed as his boss did, and, as time passed, even began picking up his boss's speech mannerisms and gestures.

He worked hard, kept his nose to the proverbial grindstone, and collected his check on payday. When Friday rolled around, George fought the traffic home and collapsed in his easy chair. Practically before he had time to blink, it was Monday morning again, time to rise before dawn and fight the traffic at sunrise to and clock in by 8:30.

Deep down, what George really wanted was to be his own boss. He wanted his own business, his own office, his own employees. There was only one minor detail: he had no cash to invest in a business of his own.

George knew there was money available for new businesses. He also knew he was not creditworthy for a conventional business loan. His application had already been turned down by two banks and a savings and loan.

Despite his situation, George now has a successful business of his own.

Donna wanted to be her own boss, too. It wasn't so much that she was fed up with her current job; what she really wanted was to start a business in a field in which she had a keen personal interest. In short, she was looking for a way to transform her hobby into a successful business.

She had a pretty good idea for a new business. She had the desire, the will, the personal courage. What she didn't have was spare cash, but like George, she had a good game plan.

Her plan was so good that within a year, for only the cost of a few postage stamps, she was grossing more than $100,000 a month.

Ed's motives were a little different. A few years ago, Ed was more interested in real estate than in starting his own business. Over time, however, he found his property investments were not paying off as dramatically as he had hoped they would. So Ed set out to investigate various alternative forms of investing. What he found was that owning a successful business

could produce bigger payouts than all of his real estate investments combined.

But, due to Ed's nature, he wanted to use other people's
money to get the business off the ground.

George, Ed, and Donna are fictitious names for real people.
All these individuals have at least three things in common: (1)
the overriding ambition to be their own bosses; (2) little or no
cash to invest; and, ultimately, (3) franchising. There is one other
thing. Each used one of the following methods to obtain the financing he or she needed:

1. A licensed Small Business Investment Company grant.
2. A Minority Enterprise Small Business Investment Company
   grant.
3. A Small Business Administration guaranteed loan.
4. A venture-capital investment.
5. Financial assistance from a franchisor.

THE FRANCHISE ADVANTAGE

Franchising is the primary reason George, Donna, and Ed
were able to get themselves into their own businesses quickly,
painlessly, and profitably. In today's franchise boom, almost
half of all U.S. domestic trade is represented by franchise
establishments. A franchise is a reduced-risk form of new business startup, with every element from site selection to inventory preplanned, carefully documented, and easily trans-
ferrable.

Three powerful influences are at play in the franchise relationship, accounting for the astonishing fact that nine out of ten
franchise businesses succeed for at least five years, whereas
eight out of ten nonfranchise startups never make it past the
first year.

The Franchisor's Success Formula

The reason a franchisor is in business is because he has developed a formula for success. That formula may include trade secrets, special patents, or a unique format. Invariably, it includes successful systems, methods, and techniques cultivated in many years of experience.

When an entrepreneur buys a franchise, he inherits the franchisor's legacy of a finely tuned business format, a meticulously documented system, and a proven product or service. He also acquires know-how and insight that would otherwise take years to assimilate.

The Franchisor's Negative Experience

A franchise has value, above and beyond the price of getting into the business, because the franchisor has invested considerable time and money developing a successful business format. In addition to his trade secrets, methods, and systems, he has also accumulated negative know-how. In other words, he not only knows what to do, but also what not to do, in order to be successful in his particular business, industry, or trade.

A franchise buyer thus avoids the trial-and-error pitfalls that normally doom a startup business to failure.

Strength in Numbers

The most obvious advantage of a franchise over other independent small businesses is the cooperative nature of the business. The franchise trade name, product, or service, and the combined purchasing power of all the outlets in the system place the franchise owner on a par with industry giants.

Hence, a franchisee is generally more competitive, more recognizable, and more profitable than other small business owners in his trading area.

There is yet another reason that George and Donna and Ed decided on a franchise to launch their American dream of self-management and independence. Because more than 90% of franchises succeed, they are the most favored of all new businesses when it comes to financing.

SBIC FUNDING

A Small Business Investment Company, or SBIC, is typically a venture capital group, investment firm, or other financial organization licensed by the federal government to invest in small, independent businesses. The government acts as a silent partner in the investment, encouraging the infusion of seed, startup, and expansion capital in new enterprises run by small time operators.

Some SBICs specialize in particular businesses or industries, including franchises.

MESBIC FUNDING

The Minority Enterprise Small Business Investment Company, or MESBIC, is a special version of the SBIC focusing on small businesses run by members of a minority group.

Where these venture capital firms are concerned, a successful franchise and a minority partner or owner make for a powerful funding formula.

SMALL BUSINESS ADMINISTRATION GUARANTEES

The SBA has been on the political ropes every year since 1984, but as of this book's publication, is still officially in the business of assisting small businesses and small business owners. The agency's most recognizable form of assistance is its power to guarantee loans to qualifying entrepreneurs for the startup, sustenance, or expansion of their small, independent businesses.

To qualify for an SBA-guaranteed loan, you must first be turned down by at least three conventional lending sources. By virtue of their survival rate, franchises are the most likely types of small businesses to qualify for assistance.

VENTURE CAPITAL

There is more venture capital available today than at any time in history. Most venture capitalists are on the lookout for new business startups, as opposed to funding the expansion of existing businesses. A firm in this business is apt to specialize in one or more fields. Some deal exclusively in or with preference to franchises.

FRANCHISOR FINANCIAL ASSISTANCE ——————————

As part of the package to ease a franchisee into the business, a large number of franchisors offer financial assistance to prospective franchise buyers. Later on, we will take a closer look at each of these important resources for financing a franchise business. But worth repeating is that every good business begins with a good plan.

EVALUATING FRANCHISES ——————————

The first step to franchising for free is deciding on a franchise. We will assume you have selected a franchise opportunity and completed a rigorous evaluation of the franchisor. Here are some key questions you probably (or should have) asked yourself as you narrowed the field:

Do you love the business? You don't necessarily have to be a Paris-trained chef to succeed in the restaurant business, or a fashion designer to prosper in the apparel trade. But it helps if you can derive both personal and professional satisfaction from the business to which you intend to devote the majority of your waking hours. It helps even more if you can have fun running it.

The franchisor will teach you the business and standardize the way it is run. But only the business itself can produce excitement, fascination, and diversion.

Does your selected franchisor have a good track record? How long has the franchisor operated a business similar to the one you are contemplating starting? How long has the company been franchising? What is the success rate among the franchises it has sold? How many outlets are under franchise agreements now? Have any franchises been repossessed, confiscated, or involuntarily terminated? If so, what were the circumstances?

Is your franchisor a good match for you?   All other factors being equal, the ideal franchisor is one whose personality and style are compatible with yours. There is an exquisite chemistry in franchising, in which both franchisor and franchisee must interact with, communicate to, and ultimately, like and respect one another.

In many respects, a franchise is a kind of partnership, with the franchisor supplying know how and the franchisee, entrepreneurial drive. Few businesses survive far beyond the point at which their partnerships turn sour.

Are you prepared to sacrifice some of your independence to improve your odds of succeeding?   Franchising is above all a mutual success formula. Your personal success depends in part on your franchisor's accumulated know how, systematized business procedures, and established network of franchise outlets. In turn, a franchisor's survival depends ultimately on the success of each and every member of the network.

But you must recognize at the outset that when you operate a franchise, you sacrifice a measure of independence in return for the franchisor's know how.

In short, evaluating a franchise means evaluating both franchisor and self. Other books and articles focus on how to *select* a franchise; this one is about financing. After you have settled on a specific franchise, or perhaps a narrow selection, your next task is the Franchise Business Plan. There are several reasons the plan comes into play so early.

First, it will provide a format for organizing your thoughts and evaluating your objectives. It will help you determine exactly how to set up the business. Moreover, it will aid you in assessing the feasibility of the business and give you a realistic snapshot of its potential performance.

Second, a franchise business plan will result in a concise, organized proposal ready to submit to a funding, lending, or investing source. It will contain all the key sections, in a readable and informative format, to answer the questions most likely to be asked about your proposed business. It will also provide the hard data that financial decision makers will require to evaluate the loan, grant, or investment.

Third, it will produce a blueprint for your business, complete with organization, marketing plan, and budget. Even after the business has been funded, the plan will guide you along the tortuous path to profitability with a lucid perspective of the factors that influence income and expenses.

The plan consists of the following essential sections:

BUSINESS STATEMENT

This section of the franchise business plan defines the business, the product, and the customer. The discussion focuses on the franchise system and its particular success formula.

It constitutes the "hook" of the business proposal, and requires both a colorful narrative and a "power" vocabulary.

This section also summarizes the industry in which the franchise business will be engaged. Here, facts and figures are important, emphasizing size, growth, dynamics, and earnings.

MARKETING PLAN

The marketing plan documents how the business will market its goods or services to its customers. It includes an analysis of the market, a profile of the customer, and a media strategy.

As a subset, an advertising plan substantiates the business's preparedness to tackle the marketplace.

MANAGEMENT PLAN

The management plan describes your personal credentials and the qualifications of your management team. It includes an

organizational matrix describing which members handle each
of the key result areas that contribute to success.

FINANCIAL FORECAST ———————————————

This section of your Franchise Business Plan documents the
business's future performance. Based on sales goals and cost estimates, a proforma operating statement predicts three years of
income and expenses, pinpointing both periodic and cumulative
cash flow.

PAYBACK ANALYSIS ———————————————

Before you submit your venture proposal to prospective investors, you must determine precisely how much cash you will
need to start the business and sustain it until it begins to turn a
profit. You must also decide on a payback plan, based on the
present value of the investment and an attractive internal rate of
return.

  This section provides a paragraph-by-paragraph guide to organizing, constructing, and wording the plan for your franchise.
The instructions and examples are based on actual financial proposals developed from case histories.

2

The
Business

In this chapter, we begin a detailed odyssey through the construction of a convincing Franchise Business Plan for a franchise business. The proposal will consist of several parts, each of which represents an important stage of planning.

The first part is the business statement.

THE BUSINESS STATEMENT

Unlike other new businesses, a franchise has a ready-made description of its business, market, and customer. Every franchisor is required by law to furnish you with a Uniform Franchise Offering Circular (UFOC) at least ten business days before you sign any agreement or make any payment.

This document is a detailed investment prospectus about the franchise, divulging important information about the franchisor, his predecessors, business, and management. It also

17

explains key sections of the franchise contract, which must accompany the UFOC, and contains the franchisor's audited financial statement. To begin planning the franchise business, you must have the UFOC package in your hands.

The section of the plan devoted to the business statement consists of the following basic parts:

1. **Business objectives.** The plan begins with a statement of your objectives: exactly why are you going into business for yourself? What do you hope to accomplish? How and when do you plan to do it?

2. **Business description.** This part contains a description of the business in which your company will be engaged, focusing on the product/service mix.

3. **Franchise description.** This part describes the franchise organization, focusing on your franchisor's track record, credentials, and benefits.

4. **Product description.** This part expands on your product or service, exploring typical applications and customer groups.

5. **Customer description.** In this part of the proposal, you define the customer for your business's products and services, describing past, present, and future demand trends.

THE OBJECTIVES OF YOUR BUSINESS

Every franchise financial proposal has four basic objectives: (1) to obtain financing, (2) to establish, develop, and open the business, (3) to capture a share of the market, and (4) to realize a profit. Hence, your business already has a financial objective, a management objective, a marketing objective, and a profit objective.

The financial objective simply states the amount of financial assistance you are seeking and the reasons. As the leading sentence in the body of the business plan, the statement of your financial objectives is the hook that will draw the reviewer. Your plan will be only one in a mountainous stack of financial proposals; the person who pores through this stack will decide which ones will be realistically considered by reading only the first few paragraphs of each one.

In the part of the plan dedicated to the financial objective, you must state two things:

1. State the amount of financial assistance you are seeking.

The sum should reflect the difference between the working capital you have available (if any) and the total amount of working capital you will need to purchase the franchise and start, develop, open, and operate the business before it begins to turn a profit.

The franchisor's UFOC should contain an estimate of your initial financial requirements in section 7 (Franchisee's Estimated Initial Investment Breakdown). However, bear in mind that this estimate is based on general estimates and averages, and may reflect the costs of doing business in the franchisor's own trading area. As a result, the initial investment breakdown most likely needs to be modified according to your local economic conditions.

The financial requirements contained in the UFOC may, but do not necessarily, contain an estimate of working capital. In this context, "working capital" means enough money to sustain the business until the break-even point. If a figure for working capital has not been included, you may have to leave the amounts in your financial objective figure blank until you have completed a financial forecast.

2. State the purpose of the financial assistance.

Describe how the money will be used and what results are desired. Break down the sum into the amounts that will be used to *establish the business, develop* it, and *provide working capital* for a specified period. That period is the estimated time that it will take your business to begin turning a profit.

Example

> Dallas Productions is seeking $175,000 with which to establish and develop a mobile video production business, under a franchise agreement with Go-Video, Inc. The sum will be used to purchase the franchise, acquire a specially retrofitted mini-van, establish a base of operations, and sustain the business for a period of six months.

———————

Note that, in this example, the business's management objectives—that is, "to purchase the franchise" and "establish a base of operations"—are integrated with the statement of financial objectives.

Besides your financial and management objectives, you must describe a marketing objective and a profit objective.

A marketing objective typically takes the form of an estimated market share. The market depends on the nature of the franchise and the size of its protected territory or, if there is no protected territory, the effective trading area. The share of that market depends in part on the number of competitors and their relative strengths.

In a large market with numerous competitors, your estimated market share may be as small as two percent. In a smaller area, such as a neighborhood, it may be as high as fifty percent or greater. As a franchise owner, you should expect to at least double the market share of competitors which are not franchise outlets. Your share relative to other franchises should be proportionate to your franchisor's relative sales compared to other franchisors in the same business.

As a rule of thumb, your marketing objective should not be less than 100 percent divided by the total number of competitors. For example, let us say you want to open a doughnut shop franchise in a town which already has twenty doughnut shops. Your minimum objective should be a five percent market share. But realistically, the town's market share will not be evenly distributed among competition.

In practice, the most dominant competitors will do two or three times as well as the average outlet. As a franchise, your outlet will out-produce the average competitor by at least 20 percent. Hence, a realistic estimate of your actual market share as a franchisee would be five percent times 1.2, or six percent of the citywide doughnut market. If your franchisor is dominant in its field, your estimated market share in this example might be as high as ten or even fifteen percent.

Example

> Our marketing objective is to capture a ten percent share of the Dallas-Fort Worth market for video production services within two years.

The last component of your statement of objectives is the business's profit objective. This figure must be left blank for now, because it will be derived from your financial forecast. In its final form, this objective will be expressed something like the following:

Example

> It is anticipated that the business will reach the break-even point after six months, realizing a small pretax profit of $8,200 at the end of the first fiscal year; and growing to $36,450 in pretax profits at the end of the second year; and $58,100 by the third.

YOUR BUSINESS _____

The next section of the business statement is a description of the proposed business. The business objectives tell where you are going; the business statement tells where you are now. It has two parts: a business summary and a business history.

Your franchisor's UFOC should contain a description of the franchise business in section 1(d) (Franchisee's Business). However, this dry, colorless overview of your newfound enterprise will have to undergo a dramatic metamorphosis.

Figure 1 shows a sample description of a franchise business extracted from a sample UFOC. This description, however accurate, is hardly enticing enough to attract the notice of a venture capitalist or loan officer. As with most of the franchisor's documentation, the UFOC is constructed with verbage that stresses the franchisor's point of view, but does little to elaborate on the franchisee's circumstances.

As you re-word the business description, use a "power" vocabulary rich in evocative, emotion-charged terms. For example, try adjectives that connote action, technology, future, uniqueness, and progress. Here are some examples:

active	innovative
aggressive	original
animated	patented
copyright	performance
creative	potent
customized	powerful
demonstrated	priority
dynamic	productive
electric	proven
energetic	scientific
guaranteed	technological
high-powered	unique
high-technology	vigorous
ingenious	

Figure 1

Example of a UFOC
Description of a Franchise Business

d. *Description of Franchisee's Business.*   Each Franchisee will operate the Go-Video System as an independent business utilizing the Go-Video name, marks, business concept and the System Unit developed by Go-Video, Inc. The Franchisee will offer and provide only the following services and products to the general public and to businesses in his/her market: video production, editing, duplication, film and slide transfer, and videotape and case sales.

No other services or products may be offered by the Franchisee without the prior written approval of Go-Video, Inc. [F.A.1] [F.A.4(B)]

e. *Competition.*   Go-Video is unaware of any company providing complete production and on-line editing services from a vehicle specifically customized, designed and retrofitted for that purpose in any other market, that could compete with a Go-Video System on a price/value basis.

Neither the Franchisor nor its predecessors have previously offered franchises of any type in this line of business or in any other business. This is the initial franchise offering.

2. IDENTITY AND BUSINESS EXPERIENCE OF PERSONS AFFILIATED WITH THE FRANCHISOR:

R. Terren Dunlap, President and Director

1983–Present: President and Director of Go-Video, Inc. With his partner, Mr. Lang, was responsible for the research, development and market testing of the complete Go-Video System; has direct experience in video production operations; participated in planning and promotion of the Company's successful public stock offering in 1986; and is responsible for corporate management— legal, financial and public affairs and video production operations.

1982–1983: Officer and Director, American Videogram, Inc., Scottsdale, Arizona. With Mr. Lang, conducted market research, and developed and executed marketing plans for a major video marketing client.

1980–1982: Chief Executive Officer of Dunlap Forest Products, Scottsdale, Arizona. In charge of marketing, he took company to $1.3 million in sales in second year of operation.

1975–1979: Engaged in the practice of law. Carson, Messinger, Elliot, Laughlin & Ragan—Phoenix, Arizona. Concentration was in the practice of corporate, partnership and business law.

Private practice—Mansfield, Ohio. Concentration was in . . .

Briefly describe the nature of the business and its principal office address. If the office address is the same as your residence, use that.

Example

Go-Video is in the business of selling video production services and products to the general public, as well as to businesses and institutions. The Go-Video concept revolves around an innovative, mobile video production studio housed in an ergonomically designed, attractive mini-van. Every piece of equipment and every element of production has been streamlined and optimized to enable quick, convenient, professional production and editing services at almost any client location.

For a base hourly price or packaged flat rate, a client receives all of the elements involved in a custom video production, including lighting and sound equipment, a character generator for titles, broadcast-quality camera equipment, monitors, mixers, and special effects and sound dubbing facilities.

In addition, the client receives the services of a Certified Video Systems Operator (VSO) and an assistant VSO.

BUSINESS HISTORY

Besides a description, the statement should also contain a history. Every business has a history, even a new one. It might be your work history, or the history of your personal involvement in the industry or trade, culminating in your decision to purchase a franchise. Beyond that, there are certain concrete actions and specific dates which give substance to the history.

Begin with your personal history, the portions of your background and experience that qualify you to own and operate a business of your own. State the time when you first became interested in the industry, and document any relevant work experience that may contribute to your likelihood of success. Supplement your personal history with a few statements about the history of the industry.

Finally, state the specific dates and actions that you have already taken to found and develop the business. Start with the date on which you were approved for a franchise. If you have taken any other steps, such as obtaining a fictitious name permit or business license, mention those dates.

Write the history, and all parts of the proposal, in the third person: "Mr. Smith" or "Ms. Johnson," not "I" or "me." Don't worry about trying to write the Great American Novel; be brief, concise, and descriptive. Above all, use good grammar and correct spelling. Nothing repels a venture capitalist faster than an illiterate business plan. On the other hand, if your writing is too flamboyant or egocentric, your proposal will get deep-sixed in five seconds.

State the facts simply, without error, misstatement, or confusion, but with as much color and appeal as you can muster.

Example

Dallas Productions was established in August, 1987 by John R. Teller. Mr. Teller, a graduate of Baylor University's broadcast communications program, has an extensive background in video engineering and production. In July, he received a commitment from Go-Video, Inc. to establish a franchise in the Dallas-Fort Worth market. Also that month, he obtained a business license and selected a site for the operation.

THE FRANCHISOR

Follow your business description with a similar description of your franchisor.

The franchisor's disclosures are contained in the UFOC in section 1. (The franchisor and its predecessors). For the most part, the description may be "lifted" with little revision, but with some important data added.

Figure 2 shows an example of a typical franchisor's description from a UFOC.

Although the UFOC description is adequate, it is usually redundant and does not include enough information to provide a complete snapshot of the franchisor's track record. Take out the superfluous parts, and add the following data:

1. **The number of franchisees sold and currently open.** This information is documented in section 20 of the UFOC (Information regarding franchisees of the franchisor).

2. **The term of the franchise.** The term, or length, of the franchise agreement is normally stated in Section 17 of the UFOC (Renewal, Termination, Re-Purchase, Modification and Assignment of the Franchise Agreement and related information).

3. **A description of the franchisor's training program.** This information is usually documented in section 11 of the UFOC (Obligations of franchisor; other supervision, assistance, or services).

Example

Go-Video has been involved in the video trade almost as long as there has been a video trade. Over a decade ago, the company's founders were creating marketing campaigns for cable television suppliers and producing live concert events. In 1982, they joined forces to conduct market research and develop marketing strategies for a major video marketing enterprise. A year later, they combined their experience in corporate marketing, business strategies, and audio-video systems to cofound Go-Video, Inc.

Figure 2

Example of a Typical Franchise Description from a UFOC

THE GO-VIDEO FRANCHISE OFFERING CIRCULAR FOR PROSPECTIVE FRANCHISEES

1. THE FRANCHISOR AND ITS PREDECESSORS:

a. *Identification & Location.* The Franchisor is Go-Video, Inc., an Arizona corporation, doing business under its corporate name with its principal business address located at 4141 No. Scottsdale Road, Suite 204, Scottsdale, Arizona 85251-3940. Its business telephone number is (602) 481-2900.

b. *History of the Franchisor.* Go-Video, Inc. (the "Franchisor") was incorporated May 16, 1984 but was doing business under the name Go-Video as a partnership for approximately six months prior to incorporation.

Prior to April of 1985 the Franchisor had its principal business address at 7064 1st Avenue, Scottsdale, Arizona 85251. In March of 1985 it moved to 4160 No. Craftsman Court, Suite 201, Scottsdale, Arizona 85251, and in November of 1986 it will move to the address shown in paragraph a. above.

c. *Description of the Franchisor's Business.* Go-Video is in the business of selling video production, duplication, editing, and production direction services, as well as blank videotape cassettes and cases, to businesses and to the general public. They are also involved in pre-production planning and script writing. They have developed and hold a patent application for a dual-port videotape cassette recorder ("VCR") and intend to license the manufacturing and marketing rights to this device. The Company is also engaged in offering franchises to qualified applicants for the Go-Video Franchise. [F.A.1]

The Go-Video concept features a complete mobile video production studio housed in a customized mini-van. The customized mini-van is called the "System Vehicle". The System Vehicle, retrofitted with video production and on-line editing, along with the video camera and accessory equipment, constitutes a "System Unit". The concept, Franchise, System Unit and the business conducted therewith constitutes the Go-Video "System". The System provides quick, convenient, professional production and editing services at almost any location the client chooses and packages the complete video production on the spot. The System uses the VHS format and one-half or three-quarter inch videotape, but can produce copies in the Beta format if desired.

27

The heart of the Go-Video concept is the Go-Video System Unit, a self-contained production studio on wheels. Within each retrofitted mini-van is a complete video production and editing facility equipped with the same state-of-the-art professional equipment used by the most sophisticated video taping establishments.

Go-Video began franchising in December, 1986. Franchisees receive comprehensive training in video production and business management at the Go-Video Learning Center in Scottsdale, Arizona. In addition, a field representative provides on-site assistance during the Grand Opening period. The term of the franchise is 5 years.

PRODUCT DESCRIPTION

The next part of the business statement is your description of the business's products and services. In the previous descriptions, you have summarized your products, but here you must delineate them in more detail.

List your product/service mix by range, category, or article. Briefly describe the attributes, including price, of each. For instance, if you will be in the food service business, describe the orientation of your outlet, the types of meals served, and the general price range. If your business will sell clothing or hardware or computers, list high-, medium-, and low-end categories, along with their applications.

Example

The Go-Video product/service mix currently includes the following basic categories:

1. Video production services
2. Video editing services

3. Videotape duplication services
4. Film-to-tape and slide-to-tape transfers
5. Videotape and cases sales

CUSTOMER DESCRIPTION _____

The business statement concludes with a description of your primary customer groups. Exactly who are the customers for the products and services of your proposed business? If they are consumers, what are their average ages, educational and income levels, residential locations? If your customers are businesses and institutions, of what type, size, and revenue level are they? How many of your business's primary customers are there in your franchise territory or trading area?

_____

Example

The market for Go-Video products and services may be viewed in three categories:

1. Consumer
2. Commercial
3. Institutional

Individuals have used Go-Video services to document special events, such as a wedding or bar mitzvah; to record their possessions for insurance purposes; and to memorialize occasions of historical family interest.

Businesses of all types use video production to create videotapes for public and financial relations, new product introductions, staff orientation and training, and documentation of seminars, meetings, and presentations.

The institutional market comprises schools, hospitals and other medical facilities, professional associations, and government agencies that have occasion to use video production services for training, communication, and documentation purposes.

The examples in this chapter illustrate an important principle in writing the business statement: numbers are important. The more markets and customers you can describe, the more attractive the business idea will appear to a prospective financial backer. Dollar amounts, dates, quantities, markets, and customers, all contribute to the "hook" that will motivate a venture capitalist or loan officer to turn past the first page of your franchise financial plan.

3

The
Market

Many businesses with a great deal of potential never become adequately funded and, as a result, are almost doomed to failure even before they open their doors. An important reason they never receive the financial backing they may deserve is poor market planning. It takes more than good people and good ideas to convince a financier to stake a startup: it also takes a good understanding of the marketplace.

Backers invest in businesses which have carefully documented market plans, brimming with accurate details about markets, customers, competitors, and costs.

Often, a business owner lumps advertising, promotion, and sales together and says all these constitute marketing. Yet another may insist that marketing and sales are two words for the same thing.

In reality, marketing may include advertising and sales but is more than both combined. The sales effort focuses on the products and services of the seller; marketing concentrates on the needs of the customer. The reason financial backers are so interested in marketing plans is that they know that a company that fails to perceive the changing needs of customers runs a high risk of failure.

The objective of the marketing plan is to explain what your products are and who your customers will be. Normally, a well conceived marketing plan requires months of study, survey, and analysis, not to mention a hearty expenditure. But someone planning a franchise business has a special advantage. The franchisor has already done a great deal of this toilsome legwork. In most cases, the franchisor knows who the primary customers of the business are, what they use the product for, and how best to reach them. What remains is for the prospective franchisee to apply these broad concepts to the much smaller market which the franchise business will attack.

The marketing plan focuses on five topics:

1. Your products and services.
2. Your markets.
3. Your customers.
4. Your competition.
5. Your advertising.

PRODUCT SERVICES MIX

The first step is to define your products and services exactly. It is not enough to state simply that your franchise will sell "computers" or "printing services" or "lodging accommodations." On the other hand, saying you will sell "AT&T Model 630 computers" or "20-pound white bond paper copies punched with three holes" is too specific.

The product mix is a description, by category, of the business's incoming-producing inventory or activities. No business sells just one item, even though a single product line may be a company's primary focus. In reality, every business sells several different things, even if they are simply accessories or replacement parts or warranty service.

For instance, a typical computer dealer derives most of his

income from selling hardware. But he also sells software, accessories, supplies, and training classes. In a similar vein, a hotel may generate most of its revenues from renting rooms, but it also sells food, beverages, banquet services, and convention services.

Create a product mix by listing precise categories, but do not name brands, makes, or models, unless they are unique or somehow integral to the franchise success formula. Here are some product classes to consider:

> Primary products
> Peripheral products
> Accessories
> Supplies
> Warranty, repair, support services
> Customer education or training
> Packaging/delivery

Include every area from which the business will actually derive income, no matter how small the amount may seem.

MARKET ANALYSIS

The next step is to identify the basic customer groups from which the business will derive its income. There are three basic categories of customer groups:

1. Consumers
2. Businesses
3. Institutions

Start by estimating the percentage of the franchise's gross revenues that will be derived from each of these sources. The franchisor should have this information at his fingertips, based on his own experience, plus the experience of other franchisees.

Very often, a business will derive all, or nearly all, of its income from just one of these primary groups. However, this fact alone does not simplify the problem of identifying the market.

In a market analysis, the focus is not on the customer as much as the customer's application. Customer analysis comes into play later on. Whereas a customer analysis asks: What customers use our company's products? A market analysis asks: What uses do people have for our company's products? What products do people want?

Market Identification: Horizontal versus Vertical Markets

Markets are traditionally viewed in two categories or, more accurately, two directions. One category consists of horizontal markets, the most obvious and therefore the primary application for the company's product. The second category is made up of the company's vertical markets, the more highly specialized needs that the company's products serve.

To envision the difference between horizontal and vertical markets, consider a franchise which has a very wide range of markets. Assume, for the sake of illustration, that you are planning to start a franchise to sell videotaping services. The primary application for videotaping services is product promotion. Hence, your horizontal market is made up of businesses who have products to promote or who are in the business of promoting products for others. The list of customers in this market includes manufacturers, wholesalers, retailers, and advertising agencies, to name a few.

However, other customers may have a need for videotaping services besides businesses. One way you might go about analyzing your market would be to conduct a small survey asking a hundred people the following question: What services do you want from video production companies? Most likely, about one third would say they wanted to record a wedding ceremony. One fifth might say they wanted to record a party, and one tenth, a sporting event. Assume your sample survey produces twenty applications in all, ranging from bar mitzvahs to music recitals. You now have a list of vertical markets for videotaping services.

Your market description is no longer limited to just "businesses" or "consumers." It now enumerates specific market segments with highly defined needs. In our example, there is a wedding market and a bar mitzvah market and a music recital market.

Once you know what customers will use your product for, you have a better understanding of precisely who they are. Business markets are not usually as difficult to define. One has only to identify a type of business to imagine a potential application for a given product.

Below is a list of vertical market categories for business customers. Look over the list and identify specific categories which represent potential customers for your franchise's products or services. Transfer the identified categories into a vertical market list of your own.

The list will be one of the exhibits in your marketing plan, so be thorough but accurate. Don't include a market category if its potential application is marginal or far-fetched.

Accounting/bookkeeping
Advertising and public relations
Agribusinesses
Banking
Business services
Counseling
Design
Distribution/wholesaling
Electronics
Engineering
Finance
Food service
Hospitality and lodging
Industrial engineering
Industrial training
Investment
Law practice
Manufacturing
Medical/dental practice
Real Estate
Retailing
Warehousing/storage

Institutional Markets

Not-for-profit entities deserve a classification separate from businesses. Even though an institution such as a government agency may have similar needs to a business, the institutional customer has different "buying behavior." It purchases products and pays for them with a different method, frequency, and decision-making process.

Here are some typical institutional markets you may wish to include in your market analysis.

Public education
Health care
Government administration
Military entities

With a list of specific markets for your proposed business's products and services, you are properly equipped for attacking the customer analysis.

CUSTOMER ANALYSIS

The customer analysis evaluates the market in relation to two things: geography, and demography. A geographic analysis asks: Exactly where do the business's customers come from? What region? State? City? Section of the city? A demographic analysis asks: Exactly who are the business's customers? What is their average age? Marital status? Average income? Hobbies and interests?

This information will help you target your promotions to the business's most likely customer groups. It will also aid in the selection of media and the planning of promotions and activities.

Geographic Analysis

Geography is often the easiest thing to identify. If your franchise will have a predefined territory, most of your customers will come from within its boundaries. However, you should be aware that franchisors may not legally restrict franchisees from selling to customers outside their franchise territories. So, a certain percentage of your business may be derived from customers beyond the geographic market granted by your franchisor.

In many businesses, particularly food and retail operations, location may mean the difference between success and failure. Products often cater to certain areas within a city. For example, a budget furniture store derives most of its business from the inner city or lower income neighborhoods, whereas a Scandinavian import store draws more heavily from outlying suburbs and upper income neighborhoods.

But a lodging establishment's customers will obviously come from a wide geographic base that will be more difficult to define. However, your chamber of commerce or your franchisor may be able to provide you with meaningful statistics.

The simplest way to express a geographic analysis is with a pie chart as in Figure 3.

Demographic Analysis of Consumers

Your customers' "demographics" are a composite of their physical, educational, cultural, and behavioral traits. For instance, it may be useful to know whether more men than women buy your product, or vice versa. If you also know the age, education level, and income of a typical customer, you will have a more explicit idea of how to advertise. For example, although more men than women read newspapers, the advertisements are read mostly by women. More middle-aged men listen to all-news radio stations during the morning commute hour than any other group, but more housewives listen to easy listening stations between 10 A.M. and noon. So, knowing where to advertise starts with knowing your customer's demographics.

Your franchisor has probably already conducted detailed customer surveys to determine these important traits. Request a copy of the franchise customer's "demographic profile" to use in your marketing plan. Figure 4 is an illustration of a typical demographic analysis.

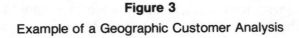

Figure 3

Example of a Geographic Customer Analysis

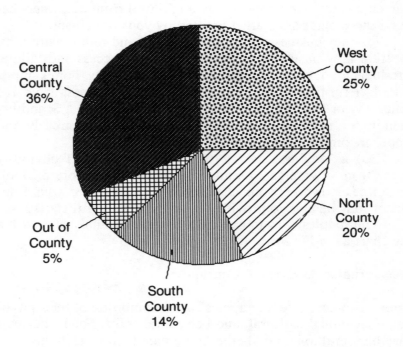

Besides these basic customer traits, the analysis might also pinpoint attributes which have a special bearing on the product or market, such as "own VCRs" or "read travel magazines." In addition, you may wish to know what sources customers consult before making a final decision, as well as the factors that enter into the decision. Do they ask friends for advice? Consult books or catalogues? Is price the most important factor? Or is it bra..d recognition, or some other quality?

Consider the following items:

Sex

Age

Figure 4

Example of a
Demographic Customer Analysis

Sex
Male	60.4
Female	39.6

Age
18–24	7.5
25–34	19.7
35–44	51.7
45–54	13.0
55 +	8.1

Income
Under $15,000	2.0
$15,001–30,000	29.5
$30,001–45,000	43.4
Over $45,000	25.1

Marital Status
Married	66.7%
Single	33.3

Income
Education
Related products owned
Related books or magazines regularly read
Related exhibitions or trade shows visited
Sources consulted prior to the purchase
Factors influencing the decision to buy

Identifying Business Customers

If individual customers have demographics, what do business customers have? They have key decision makers. If your franchise will sell to business customers, you must identify the people who will make the decision to purchase your product.

The following list enumerates some typical business customers:

Corporate training departments
Corporate marketing departments
Corporate personnel departments
Manufacturers
Realtors
Attorneys
Stock brokers
Retail businesses
Advertising agencies
Public relations agencies
Insurance companies
Clubs and associations
Small business owners
Engineers

COMPETITION ANALYSIS

Check out your competition. Know who your major competitors are, what types of services and products they offer, their prices, and how they operate.

Familiarize yourself with your competitors' sales styles, methods of presentation, and prices. Review their advertising, media, and publicity. Keep a file of all your competitors. Store copies of their ads, price lists, and a description of their services. Also, keep clippings or brochures.

A simple way to check out the competition is to call each competitor, assuming the role of a prospective customer. Note the nature and extent of the information you receive, and request catalogs, price lists, or promotional literature. Ask them how they stack up in the local area. Who's number one? Numbers two and three? What percentage of the market have they captured?

If your competition is a major chain or another franchise, your own franchisor should know their relative market share.

Again, a simple pie diagram (Fig. 5) is the most effective way of expressing a competitive analysis.

THE MARKETING BUDGET

Some franchises are more promotion-oriented than others. However, every business, including franchise businesses, engage in some form of marketing and sales promotion. The nature and extent of the marketing activity are guided in large part by the budget.

A budget should be established for each area from which

Figure 5

Example of a Competitive Market Share Analysis

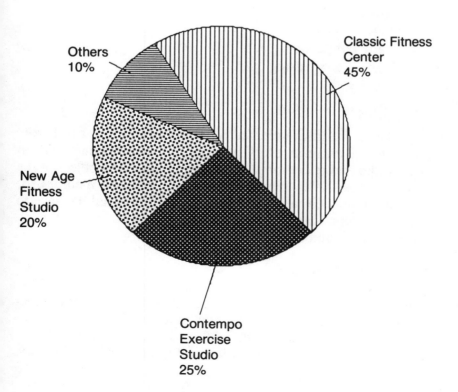

the business will derive income. The amount of the marketing budget is usually related to the gross revenues of the business. The average marketing expenditure is about 12 percent of gross sales.

If, for example, a franchise generates $200,000 per year in gross revenues, its marketing budget should be about $24,000. (This figure does not include personnel employed in strictly sales capacities.)

MEDIA ANALYSIS

The next step in creating your marketing plan is to evaluate the target advertising media in your locality. By "target" media, we mean the media used to deliver the sales promotion to your identified markets.

Here is a list of media to consider:

Major metropolitan newspapers
General interest magazines
Trade publications
Outdoor advertising
Direct mail
Electronic advertising (radio/television)

Not all media are created equal. Moreover, you can hardly afford to advertise in every newspaper and magazine, and on every radio and television station in your area. The object of the media analysis is to pinpoint the single primary medium, or handful of media, that will deliver your promotional message to your customers. Knowing who your customers are makes the job easier, but not automatic.

Newspaper Advertising

The primary advantage of newspaper advertising is that it effectively isolates prospective customers in a specific geographic locality. If, for example, a preponderantly large portion of your business will originate from a handful of areas within the city, newspaper advertising in those localities is an effective way to reach the franchise's primary target groups.

An additional advantage to newspaper advertising is that it can be placed with little advance notice, permitting rapid exposure to special promotions during unexpected slack periods.

On the downside, a newspaper ad has a short lifetime, so a campaign of frequency is usually required, compounding the media costs. Moreover, the reproduction quality is generally poor and most often limited to black and white.

Magazine Advertising

You can advertise in two types of magazines:

1. General interest
2. Specialty

The main advantage of advertising in a magazine is the ability to focus on a specific target audience. For instance, to target consumers with above average incomes, you can advertise in periodicals about travel or yachting.

Furthermore, magazine ads have a relatively long lifetime. Unlike newspapers, they tend be retained by their readers for prolonged periods, often changing hands and circulating informally above and beyond the publisher's official circulation. The superior reproduction qualities of the magazine enable the design and placement of ads of striking visual impact.

A major hindrance to magazine advertising is cost. A single ad in a major general-interest publication with a regional circulation may take a large chunk out of the franchise's entire annual ad budget.

Another drawback is the length of time required to get an ad into print. Unless you sign a frequency contract, agreeing to purchase several ads over a set period of time, a lead time of 60 days or more may be required in a monthly publication. However, weekly magazines can normally get your ad into print within two to four weeks, and most experience last-minute cancellations, freeing up a limited amount of ad space which must be filled quickly.

Trade Publications

To promote sales to training directors, personnel managers, product promoters, advertising agencies, and other commercial users, trade publications edited for businesses in your locality are also likely delivery media.
The following are examples:

Local business journals
Local or regional editions of national business journals
Corporate training publications
Personnel management publications
Advertising journals
Convention publications

Besides local business journals published for citywide or statewide distribution, some national business journals and magazines, such as *The Wall Street Journal, Newsweek,* and *Time,* have metropolitan and regional editions.

Direct Mail

Direct mail campaigns to advertise your product may also be effective in both attracting new customers and encouraging repeat business.
A list of potential customers in your area can usually be obtained from a business magazine or trade publication. Phone numbers can often be provided on request. The list can be broken down into sections, such as state, county, or zip code.
The typical cost of a direct mail campaign, including labeling, metering, handling, and postage, is about 25 cents per name.

Outdoor Advertising

Most businesses have two types of outdoor advertising at their disposal, outdoor signage and billboards. The sign that marks the business location and promotes its name to passing traffic is the typical retail business's most pronounced form of advertising.

Strategically-placed billboards may also be effective ways of reaching a captive audience of target customers trapped in cross-town traffic.

A business that operates delivery or service vehicles has another form of outdoor advertising, the decals on the sides of its trucks. A service vehicle is literally a traveling billboard touting the business's name wherever it goes.

Electronic Advertising

Radio and television advertising clearly reach the greatest audience, but at substantial cost and little ability to target specific customer groups.

The electronic media offer the advantages of strong emotional appeal and a large number of impressions generated in the marketplace. However, for the typical franchisee, the high cost per thousand impressions is severely limiting.

Radio and television campaigns are best conducted for frequency and reach, to create awareness of the business's name, rather than to create a specific response. In a typical franchise, radio and TV ads are usually paid for by the franchisor from a co-op ad fund sustained by the collective body of franchisees.

ADVERTISING BUDGET

The idea of the media analysis is to focus on your best-odds customer, assuring that few ad dollars will be wasted on prospects unlikely to consume your product. For instance, it makes little sense for a women's beauty salon to advertise in a men's outdoor magazine, or for a pizza restaurant to advertise in a diet publication.

For planning purposes, advertising expenses fall into two categories: static and programmable. A static advertising expense is a fixed cost. Your Yellow Pages advertisement is an example. A billboard is also a static advertising expense. A programmable advertising expense is one that may change with a variable such as gross sales or the cost-per-thousand impressions required to obtain a specific sales goal.

Unfortunately, sales do not remain static throughout the year. They are more likely to fluctuate from quarter to quarter, so your advertising budget should be finely tuned to this fluctuation. Your franchisor should be able to provide you with very accurate statistics regarding seasonal sales fluctuations. Each quarter should be expressed as a percentage of the year's total sales.

For example, the following seasonal pattern has been observed by a franchisor in the office equipment business:

January through March	15 percent of annual sales
April through June	25 percent of annual sales
July through September	25 percent of annual sales
October through December	35 percent of annual sales

Once you know the pattern for your business, you should allocate advertising expenses according to these quarterly percentages. As your business history grows and you accumulate sales data of your own, you will be able to adjust your advertising budget to reflect the quarterly sales percentages of your franchise.

A simple method of budgeting annual ad expenditures is to set aside a percentage of gross revenues. For your local advertising budget, 6 to 12 percent may be considered adequate. During your initial startup period, your ad budget may be as high as 20 percent of sales.

For example, if your projected annual sales are $600,000, your annual ad budget at 6 percent would amount to $36,000. Based on the quarterly percentages shown in the foregoing example, this budget would be allocated as follows:

January through March	$ 5,400	(15%)
April through June	9,000	(25%)
July through September	9,000	(25%)
October through December	12,600	(35%)
	$36,000	(100%)

Ad Planning

An Advertising Plan will allow you to control and monitor your advertising campaigns. Your selection of media for each promotional quarter should be tied to the relative budget allocations based on your anticipated sales volume.

In general, it is best not to spread your advertising budget too thinly. Rather than attempting to advertise in every available medium on a consistent basis, you are usually better off concentrating your efforts on major campaigns conducted less frequently. Otherwise, you run the risk of diluting your promotional budget among too many media, resulting in a weak impression and a small audience.

For example, newspaper ad salesmen will invariably attempt to sell you on a "rate holder" ad; if you agree to run an ad in their paper every day, or a minimum number of days, within a month, quarter, or year, the newspaper will guarantee you a low rate.

However, the total commitment will be substantial, resulting in a drain on your ad budget and precluding effective campaigns you might otherwise have conducted in other media. As a rule, you should be wary of the "rate holder" plan.

Radio and television ad salesmen offer similar "discount" advertising plans, based on BTA (Best Time Available) slots. If you agree to purchase a specified number of spots under such a plan, the station will guarantee you a discount rate. Unfortunately, the "best time available" is not often a desirable time slot for attracting business clients or upper income demographic consumers. In fact, you have no assurance when and where your commercial will run. Usually, ads purchased on a BTA plan (sometimes called a "TAP" plan) end up adjacent to the station sign-off, 4 A.M. movie, or morning prayer.

The purchase of spots in guaranteed time slots of your selection, at a higher price per spot is preferable. The effectiveness of accurately targeting your audience far outweighs the additional cost per spot.

Figure 6 shows an example of a typical ad budget for a retail franchise. Some franchisors mandate or control ad expenditures by franchisees. Still others dictate the exact media which

Figure 6

Sample Franchise Advertising Budget

ADVERTISING BUDGET

Quarter	1 Jan–Mar	2 Apr–Jun	3 Jul–Sep	4 Oct–Dec
RADIO Morning Drive Time	2250.	1500.	2250.	3000.
TV Late Night News	1400.	700.	1400.	2800.
PRINT Tribune Sports	1000.			2000.
DIRECT MAIL	500.		500.	
QUARTERLY TOTALS %	5150. 27%	2200. 11%	4150. 22%	7800. 40%

TOTAL ANNUAL BUDGET   19,300.

you may use, or do all the ad buying for franchisees. In any event, your marketing plan must include all the items discussed in this chapter:

Market analysis
Customer analysis
Competition analysis
Advertising plan

Though your financial backer will weigh many decisions before deciding to invest in your franchise, one of the first judgments he will form will be how clearly *you* understand the marketplace.

4

The Financial Outlook

The most obvious component of every business plan is a financial forecast. Indeed, a typical executive may create a spreadsheet of predicted income and expenses and consider that a business plan. Yet this hypothetical snapshot of the company's performance is usually not so much a plan as a budget. Few planning processes are so common yet so difficult to do well as financial planning.

A franchise has special financial considerations, including factors not present in other business entities, that make its financial plan unique. And a franchise proposal has certain features on which a conventional business plan might not touch.

For the purposes of your proposal, the financial plan has three separate sections:

1. Proforma Operating Statement
2. Proforma Cash Flow Statement
3. Proforma Financial Statement

Literally translated, the Latin term proforma means "as a matter of form." In a business forecast, proforma indicates a conventional financial report using projected hypothetical data, rather than current actual data. Thus, a proforma operating statement refers to a prediction of income and expenses over a future period, rather than the company's real financial performance in the past. A proforma financial statement predicts the net worth of the owners at some future point, rather than the actual current assets and liabilities of the business.

In your franchisor's UFOC, the hypothetical profits of your future business are most likely referred to as "projected" or "forecast" earnings. Note that these are not the same as a "proforma operating statement." A franchisor's projected earnings statement is usually figured by taking an average of the earnings reported by existing franchisees. In many cases, the average is based only on franchisees in your own geographic region. In contrast, a proforma operating statement has the appearance of an actual profit-and-loss statement, including itemized estimates of operating costs and taxes.

Since your business has no history of income and expenses, no assets or liabilities, all the reports in your financial proposal will be proforma analyses.

PROFORMA OPERATING STATEMENT

An operating statement, sometimes called an income statement or profit-and-loss sheet, itemizes the business's revenues and expenses to figure the profits (or losses) for the period in question. Thus, a proforma operating statement predicts the company's profitability based on sales goals, or estimates, and the anticipated costs of doing business.

Obviously, an accurate forecast requires accurate estimates. Normally, a substantial research effort is required to estimate the future expenses of a new business. But with a typical franchise, a large body of useful information about income and expenses already exists. Unless it is a brand new effort, the franchisor's other franchisees have already undergone the difficult startup process and, usually, possess several years of financial history.

Obtain this data from your franchisor early in the planning process. Most franchisors gladly assist their franchisees with financial planning and forecasting, but usually only after the franchise agreement has been signed and a check written out for the initial fee. Unfortunately, the time when you need financial facts the most is before you sign the agreement.

Most franchisors have detailed information regarding average income and expenses of the franchise outlet at their fingertips. Ask them for it, and tell them why you want it.

Other franchisees are also potential sources of historical data. Every franchisor's Uniform Franchise Offering Circular includes a list of existing franchisees, including names, addresses, and phone numbers. The franchisor usually restricts its franchisees' ability to divulge information about the franchise, but you may be able to obtain "ball park" figures relating to certain expenses, such as inventory, fixtures, signs, and supplies. Being able to cite another franchisee as a source of your estimated business expenses will further establish credibility in the mind of your future financial backer.

The proforma operating statement is based on two main factors: *projected revenues* and *anticipated expenses*. But it must also take into consideration *cash requirements*, *debt service* (interest and loan payments), and *taxes*.

A new business begins with estimates, based on available statistics or averages for similar operations, as well as management's best estimation of sales. An established business has a wealth of historical information relating to income and expenses, enabling quite accurate forecasting and realistic budgeting.

Projecting Revenues

Thanks to your marketing plan, by now you have a pretty good handle on the business's sources of income. The first part of your proforma operating statement should list each income source and estimate the corresponding proceeds.

Estimate the actual number of products or services you believe you will sell in each month of the year. Start conservatively, showing a small figure in the first month, gradually growing from 20 to 50 percent each month thereafter in the first year, then slowing to 12 to 20 percent per month in the second. By the third year, show a flat sales performance, with neither an increase nor a decline in the number of units sold.

If your franchisor has a particular sales goal, quota, or average increase rate, use the corresponding percentages.

As an example, suppose you are planning a financial counseling business which will derive income from three sources:

Financial counseling
Estate planning
Sales of do-it-yourself last will and testament kits

Assume that this type of business takes two months to outfit and open. Hence, no sales are expected in months one and two. Further assume that in the first month in which the franchise open (month three), you expect to sell 80 hours of financial counseling services, 40 hours of estate planning services, and 50 will kits. Based on an average monthly sales increase of 20 percent, your sales forecast for the first six months would look like this:

	Month					
Unit Sales	1	2	3	4	5	6
Fin. Counseling	$0	$0	$80	$96	$115	$138
Estate Planning	0	0	40	48	58	69
Kit Sales	0	0	50	60	72	87

But what if you are considering a business which will sell many different products at varying prices? For example, an import furniture store might carry more than 300 different items, no two of which have the same exact price. Obviously, it would be impractical to list and estimate sales in every possible price category. In this case, devise a manageable set of generic price levels. You might divide your products into high end, medium, and low end price categories, and estimate unit sales in each category.

Consider, as an example, a hotel with twelve different room rates, based on view, location, bedding type, decor, and similar variables. Rather than creating a sales estimate for all fourteen rate categories, divide the hotel into three average ranges: minimum, moderate, and maximum. Compute the average rate in each category. For example, let's say the lowest four room rates are distributed as follows:

Rate	Number of Rooms at This Rate
48.00	15
52.00	25
56.00	15
60.00	20

To compute the average minimum rate, multiply each rate times the number of rooms offered at that rate. Add all the products, and divide this sum by the total number of rooms represented by all four rates. The average minimum rate would be computed in the foregoing example as:

$$
\begin{array}{rl}
\$48 \times 15 = & \$\ 720 \\
52 \times 25 = & 1300 \\
56 \times 15 = & 840 \\
60 \times 20 = & \underline{1200} \\
75 & \$4060
\end{array}
$$

$$
\frac{\$4060}{75} = \$54.13
$$

The average price of a minimum rate room in this example is $54.13. The total number of rooms at this average rate is 75.

Extend your monthly forecast to cover the first three years of business.

With a detailed sales forecast, estimating revenues is a simple arithmetic procedure. For each month of your forecast, multiply the number of units sold times the average price per unit. If your product mix involves several price levels, estimate the number of units you expect to sell at each level.

To illustrate the procedure, let us return to the example of the financial counseling franchise. Assume your services will be based on flat rates; and your average rates will be $150 for a financial counseling program and $75 for estate planning. Additionally, the price of a do-it-yourself last will and testament will be $10.

Based on your foregoing sales forecast, your projected revenues over the first six months would be:

	Month					
Revenues	1	2	3	4	5	6
Fin. Counseling	$0	$0	$12000	$14400	$17250	$20700
Estate Planning	0	0	3000	3600	4350	5175
Kit Sales	0	0	500	600	720	870
Total Revenues	$0	$0	$15500	$18600	$22320	$26745

Complete the revenue projection for your entire three-year sales forecast.

Obviously, some attention must be devoted to pricing, before sales revenues may be estimated. In many instances, determining the price at which goods will be sold to the public is not automatic. Franchisors may suggest prices but are in no position to specify them. Price fixing is one of the oldest business practices declared illegal by the U.S. Supreme Court. In short, no franchisor may attempt in any way to set, fix, encourage, discourage, or stipulate the price of any product you sell. To avoid touchy price-fixing issues, some franchisors shy away from the pricing problem altogether.

Nevertheless, pricing may well dictate your success or failure in business. Your prices must be neither so high as to turn away customers, nor so low as to sacrifice profit. Yet despite its fundamental importance to the survival and well-being of every business, the price decision is one of the least understood aspect of management.

Since, ultimately, the onus of determining prices falls on your shoulders, let us take a closer look at some of the important considerations involved in the price decision.

Pricing

The objective of pricing is to seek that exquisite point at which, with a particular sales volume, your business makes the most profit without sacrificing demand. When you determine the prices for your products, many considerations should enter into the decision besides operating expenses and cost of goods. Take into account the *nature of the product*, the *amount and influence of competition*, *local business and economic conditions*, and your *specific marketing strategy*.

A unique product may often be successfully sold at a very high margin. In contrast, you may have difficulty selling your products if they are priced higher than those charged by others in your trading area, even though you are legally free to do so. So, to some degree, your competition may influence your pricing strategy.

With these factors in mind, weigh the role of price in relation to other marketing instruments, such as advertising, packaging, product quality or distinction, and personal selling.

Two separate measures are commonly used to determine resale prices: margins and markups. The difference between the actual cost and the selling price is the "margin" or "markup." Either may be expressed as a percentage, but the two expressions are quite different.

A margin is a comparison of the selling price and the difference between the selling price and the actual cost. The following formula may be used to compute the margin:

$$\text{Margin} = \frac{\text{Actual Cost}}{\text{Selling Price}}$$

For example, if the selling price of a particular product is $50 and the actual cost is $25, the margin is computed as follows:

$$\text{Margin} = \frac{25}{50} = .50, \text{ or } 50\%$$

A markup is simply a comparison of the actual cost and the difference between the selling price and the actual cost. The following formula may be used to compute the markup:

$$\text{Markup} = \frac{(\text{Selling Price} - \text{Actual Cost})}{\text{Actual Cost}}$$

In the foregoing example, the markup is calculated as follows:

$$\text{Markup} = \frac{(50 - 25)}{25} = 1.00, \text{ or } 100\%$$

The more meaningful of the two measurements is the gross margin, which reveals how much of your sales dollar contributes to the payment of operating overhead and net profit. The following procedure provides a method of price determination based on the profit objectives of your business.

1. Establish a profit objective. Decide how much profit you expect to earn from the business. Express the profit objective as a percentage of gross sales.

2. Calculate your percentage cost of operations. Analyze the operating expenses of the business in relation to actual or forecasted gross sales. Divide total sales by total expenses to calculate the percentage cost of operations.

$$\text{Percentage Cost of Operations} = \frac{\text{Sales}}{\text{Expenses}}$$

3. Add your profit objective and the percentage cost of operations.

$$\text{Profit Objective} + \text{Percentage Cost of Operations} = \text{Margin}$$

The sum is the margin required to pay overhead and realize your profit expectations.

4. Use the following formula to determine the selling price:

$$\text{Price} = \frac{\text{Cost}}{100 - \text{Margin}} \times 100$$

For example, assume you want to determine a price for a product costing $30 at wholesale; your profit objective is 15 percent, and your cost of operations is 65 percent. The margin would therefore be 80. Your selling price would be calculated as follows:

$$\text{Price} = \frac{30}{100 - 80} \times 100 = 150$$

Estimating Expenses

The second part of the proforma operating statement is devoted to expenses. Although your franchisor, or one or more franchisees, may have supplied you with average cost estimates, many of these will have to be adjusted to local economic conditions.

The first source of expense information is the franchisor's Uniform Franchise Offering Circular. Section 7 is devoted to the franchisee's estimated initial investment. This section usually breaks down your initial costs of things like leasehold improvements, equipment purchases, inventory, deposits for utilities, and so forth. Both high and low estimates may be given. To be conservative, it is best to use the high estimates, or, if your locality has a relatively low cost of living, median figures halfway between the high and low.

The remaining expense items may be estimated with very little legwork. Following are some basic guidelines for figuring the future expenses of the business.

1. **Wages and salaries.**   Designate a salary for yourself, plus any planned salaries or wages for other employees, beginning in the month in which you plan to hire them. As an illustration, let us say you plan to pay yourself a salary of $2500 per month; at some point you will also begin depositing profits from the business, but until then your salary will let you meet your living costs during the difficult startup period. Also assume you will need an additional fulltime employee and a part-time assistant. You plan to pay the fulltime help $1750 per month and the

part-time employee $750. Your monthly salary expenses would be figured as follows:

Owner/manager	$2,500
Fulltime counselor	1,750
Part-time assistant	750
Total Salaries	$5,000

2. **Taxes and benefits.** Figure a minimum of 15 percent of the total amount of wages and salaries for payroll taxes and benefits. If you plan to offer a health insurance plan to your employees, calculate the cost of taxes and benefits at 20 to 25 percent.

For our example, take the middle ground and say your payroll taxes and benefits will be about 20 percent of salaries. If your total salary expenses are $5000 per month, your taxes and benefits would be figured as follows:

$$\text{Salaries} \times \text{Payroll Tax and Benefits} = \$5000 \times .20 = \$1000$$

In this case, you would allot $1000 per month for payroll taxes and employee benefits.

3. **Commercial space.** If you plan to operate the business at home, multiply your rent or monthly mortgage payment by 20 percent. Use this figure as an estimate of the cost of commercial space. If your business will be located in a store or office site other than your home, use the actual monthly lease or loan payment for the site.

To obtain an estimate before you have actually signed a franchise agreement, you will have to go through the motions of selecting a site. The site you choose does not necessarily have to be the exact place where your business will actually be located, but it should be comparable. Select a vacant store or office site that is suitable for the business and meets all the franchisor's specifications and criteria.

Some franchisors may insist that you open your business in a specific site. This may be the case if the franchisor has already purchased or leased real estate in your market area, and wants you to buy or sublease from him. But in other instances, it is best to select three alternative sites for the business, representing high, medium, and low cost range.

Once you have settled on a tentative site, ask the lessor to provide you with estimates of improvements and utilities. Often, these additional costs can be figured into the monthly lease or mortgage payment.

To illustrate, suppose you find a suitable office site for the business at a cost of $900 per month. The lessor pays utilities for the entire office complex and charges each tenant $120 per month for lights, power, heating and air conditioning.

Your monthly estimate of commercial space expenses would be figured as follows:

Lease payment	$ 900
Utilities	120
Total Space Lease	$1,020

4. **Communications.** The communications expenses of the business include your monthly phone bill and the cost of postage.

To estimate your monthly phone bill, contact your local telephone company. Double the monthly service charge to allow for long distance calls to suppliers. For example, if the monthly charge for business service in your locality is $60, figure your telephone expenses as follows:

$$\text{Telephone Cost} \times 2 = \$60 \times 2 = \$120$$

To figure your communications expenses, add an estimated cost for postage. Obviously, some businesses use the mail more than others. For the purposes of illustration, estimate that your business will spend about $120 per month on postage and shipping. Your monthly communications estimate would be figured as follows:

Telephone expense	$120
Postage/shipping	120
Total communications	$240

5. **Advertising.** Estimate your advertising budget based on the ad plan you devised earlier. Be sure to cover the following items in your advertising estimate:

Monthly cost of Yellow Page advertising
Grand Opening costs
Cost of printing fliers, shown in Month One
Monthly cost of newspaper, radio, or television ads

If your ad plan is based on quarterly expenditures, you can do either of two things. For one, you might divide the ad budget for each quarter into three equal amounts to distribute monthly. Say your ad budget for the first quarter is $3144. Your monthly advertising expenses for the first three months of the fiscal year would be figured as follows:

$$\frac{\text{Quarterly Ad Budget}}{3} = \frac{\$3144}{3} = \$1048$$

In this example, you would show an advertising estimate of $1048 in each of the first three months. If your ad budget for the second quarter is $2244. For the fourth, fifth, and sixth months of the fiscal year, your advertising expenses would be estimated as follows:

$$\frac{\text{Quarterly Ad Budget}}{3} = \frac{\$2244}{3} = \$748$$

For the remaining months, substitute the appropriate figure for the quarterly ad budget.

As an alternative, you might simply show the total quarterly budget in the first month of each quarter, leaving the remaining months at zero. In the example above, you would show an advertising expense of $3144 in the first month, zero in the second and third, $2244 in the fourth, and zero in the fifth and sixth.

In reality, some of your advertising expenses will be paid out monthly (for example, Yellow Page advertising). Others will be paid out as lump sums (the cost of printing fliers or placing an ad on the radio). It may be worth your extra effort to detail the ad plan month by month, rather than using quarterly allowances or averages. Financial backers are interested in the real status of your cash flow at the end of every month. The more accurate your itemized monthly expenses, the more realistic your cash flow projection will be.

6. **Travel and expenses.** If your business will require travel, estimate the number and cost of trips. Use this category to estimate the cost of business lunches, receptions, or other entertainment expenses, as well.

Because accuracy is important, if you know the specific destinations or events, use real air fares, hotel rates, catering bids, etc., to calculate your estimate. Write down each item included in your travel expense estimate, so that you can justify the figure in the operating statement.

7. **Legal/accounting services.** Estimate the cost of legal and accounting services for such expenses as producing financial statements, calculating tax liability, and organizing the business. If you plan to use an outside bookkeeping service, include the fee quoted by your chosen vendor.

Count on two visits with an attorney each year. Even though you might not ever need to use an attorney after the business has been organized, it is wise to include a small allowance for legal services in your projection.

Average costs of professional services range from $200 to $300 per year for very small franchises to as much as $1500 to $2000 per year for a typical retail operation.

8. **Sales Commissions.** If your business involves commissioned salespeople or independent contractors, calculate the commissions for each month. First, estimate the percentage of total sales which will be generated by commissioned sales

personnel. Multiply that percentage times the sales commission to calculate the commission expenses.

9. **Insurance.** No matter what your business is or where you conduct it, you will need business liability insurance and, most likely, comprehensive motor vehicle insurance. Compute the total monthly premiums and enter the amount in your financial plan. Typically, insurance premiums are paid twice annually. The amount may range from $600 to $1800 depending on your type of business.

10. **Equipment and tools.** Estimate the monthly costs for leasing or purchasing equipment, tools, furnishings, and vehicles for the business.

   This figure may usually be derived from Section 7 of the Uniform Franchise Offering Circular.

11. **Office supplies.** To estimate the cost of office supplies for each month of your projection, multiply $50 times the number of employees.

12. **Other expenses.** Your franchise may include other expense items unique to its business or trade. For example, in a retail business, the cost of goods sold will be an important factor. That cost, as well as such items as freight, delivery, postage, etc., can usually be expressed as an actual or average percentage of gross sales.

   As you prepare your expense estimates, be thorough but conservative. You may have heard it is far better to overestimate expenses and underestimate sales than to exceed realistic expectations. However, in the case of a financial proposal, that does not really hold true. You should neither overestimate nor underestimate either sales or the cost of doing business.

Of course, evaluating the past is always easier than predicting the future. To allow for the unforeseen, your financial plan should include at least two different proforma operating statements—one depicting optimistic sales, the other a worst-case scenario.

For your own use in planning and managing the business, you are well advised to create many different forecasts, to equip yourself for handling changing sales patterns and unanticipated expenses. However, for the purposes of your financial proposal, two projections are adequate.

The nature of investors is to be optimistic but skeptical. Hence, they are equally interested in how well your business can do, as well as what might happen if something goes wrong.

The following list may help you identify the expense items to include in your financial plan. This generalized list may include items that do not pertain to your franchise, e.g., sales commissions.

Cost of sales
Wages and Salaries
Payroll Taxes and Employee benefits
Sales Commissions
Insurance
Freight
Advertising/promotion
Legal and accounting
Telephone
Custodial service
Office supplies
Postage
Licenses and taxes
Dues and subscriptions
Credit card fees
Bank charges
Travel expenses
Vehicle expenses
Maintenance supplies
Miscellaneous expenses & petty cash

To compute the actual dollar amount of each expense item, you should be aware of the difference between fixed and variable expenses.

FIXED VERSUS VARIABLE EXPENSES

The business's expenses fall into two categories: (1) fixed, and (2) variable. A fixed expense remains constant; it does not change either when sales increase or when revenues decline. A variable expense is directly related to revenue; it fluctuates with the sales volume. The following examples illustrate this difference.

Fixed	*Variable*
Salaries	Credit card fees
Yellow Pages advertising	Utilities
Insurance	Advertising
Interest expense	Cost of goods sold

A fixed expense is sometimes referred to as an "indirect cost" or "static" expense, because it rarely, if ever, varies. A variable expense is sometimes called a "direct cost" or "programmable" expense, because its value depends on sales volume.

With a fixed expense, you simply use the actual cost estimate, for example, the monthly cost of an ad in the Yellow Pages, or an insurance premium. To estimate a variable expense, you need to know the percentage of gross sales. For instance, in a hardware store, the cost of goods might be 50 percent, or in a computer store, 70 percent. The cost of processing credit card transactions might be 3 percent. To figure the variable expense, multiply the percentage times the total revenue for the month in question.

Most franchises have at least one, and usually two, very important variable expenses: the franchise royalty, and the co-op ad fund contribution. The royalty is normally based on gross sales, not profits. The term most often used by franchisors is "net revenues." But be careful not to confuse this term with "net sales," which is something entirely different. Franchise agreements usually define net revenues as the total receipts of the business, less sales tax collected, refunds, and returns. In other words, royalties are paid before expenses are deducted.

Remember to deduct sales taxes before figuring the royalty payment. The following formula offers a quick method of estimating net revenues (total sales less sales tax):

$$\text{Net Revenues} = \frac{\text{Total Sales}}{(1 + \text{Sales Tax Rate})}$$

For example, in a particular month your business deposits $119,700 from sales. Included in that amount are sales taxes collected at a rate of five percent. Net revenues would be calculated as follows:

$$\text{Net Revenues} = \frac{\text{Total Sales}}{(1 + \text{Sales Tax Rate})} = \frac{\$119,700}{(1 + .05)}$$

$$= \frac{\$119,700}{1.05} = \$114,000$$

In this example, your net revenues would be $114,000. If your royalty is also five percent, your royalty payment would be $5,700 (.05 × $114,000).

Be careful not to overlook your contribution to the franchise advertising fund, if your franchisor has one. If your monthly ad royalty is two percent, and your net revenues are $114,000, your ad royalty would be $469.16 (.02 × $114,000).

Projecting Profits

The point of all this estimating is to predict the business's profits (or losses) at any point. Subtract total expenses from total revenues, and you have your pre-tax profits for the period in question.

The traditional operating statement ends at this point. But for the purposes of your proposal, two steps remain. The first is to subtract business taxes. The second is to determine the company's cash flow.

Estimating taxes may be a bit difficult in the light of the 1986 Tax Reform Act, which radically altered the way both taxable income and taxes are computed. Despite reducing the number of taxation levels, the new law complicated many other aspects of computing tax liability.

As of July 1, 1987, there are four official tax rates for corporations, but they are levied in five different income brackets, as follows:

Taxable Income (Profits)	Tax Rate
Less than $50,000	15%
$50,000–$74,999	$7,500 + 25% of the amount over $50,000
$75,000–$99,999	$13,750 + 34% of the amount over $75,000
$100,000–$334,999	$22,250 + 39% of the amount over $100,000
$335,000 or more	34%

Besides these basic tax rates, a surcharge of 5 percent or $11,000, whichever is less, applies to taxable corporate income above $100,000.

As an example, assume the projection shows an annual profit of $45,000. Since the amount is less than $50,000, the corporate tax is 15 percent, or

$$\$45,000 \times .15 = \$6,750$$

When the business earns more than $50,000, the computation becomes more involved. For instance, if the annual pretax profit is $75,000, the corporate tax is determined as follows:

$$\$7,500 + .25(75,000 - 50,000) = \$13,750$$

With annual profits of about $100,000, remember to add the surcharge (5 percent or $11,000).

In practice, a business takes a deduction for such items as depreciation, capitalized equipment purchases, etc. If your startup includes a substantial investment in depreciable items, for example, real estate, machinery, or business vehicles, your profits and taxes should be adjusted as follows:

1. Add the purchase cost of the depreciable item to your pre-tax profit, before determining the tax.
2. Figure the depreciation, and subtract the amount from the new taxable income figure.
3. Determine the tax liability using the basic rate.

For example, in the first month, Franchisee X invests $30,000 in depreciable equipment, and depreciates the amount over five years, resulting in a $6,000 per year allowable deduction. In his first year, X does not turn a profit, but in by the end of the second, he shows a pre-tax profit of $40,000. Here is how X determines his tax liability:

1. Adjusted income = $30,000 + $40,000 = $70,000
2. Depreciation = $6,000
3. Taxable income = $64,000
4. Tax = $7,500 + .25(64,000 − 50,000) = $11,000

Subtract the total tax liability for the year from the total pre-tax profit for the year. The result is the company's net profit after taxes.

Figure 7 illustrates a proforma operating statement for a hypothetical franchise business.

PROFORMA CASH FLOW STATEMENT

The profit projection tells an investor whether the business will experience a profit or a loss in any given month. It does not, however, show the true cash position of the company. The cash flow analysis asks: How much cash will actually be on hand?

The cash flow analysis is relatively simple. Add each month's profit to the last month's profit. In months in which losses are incurred, express the loss as a negative profit.

Figure 7

Example of a Proforma Operating Statement

Year One Month	1	2	3	4	5	6
Net Sales	8400	9240	10164	11180	12298	13528
Cost of Goods	4200	4620	5082	5590	6149	6764
Total Revenues	4200	4620	5082	5590	6149	6764
Salaries	5000	5000	5000	5000	5000	5000
Taxes/Benefits	750	750	750	750	750	750
Commissions	840	924	1016	1118	1230	1353
Space Lease	1020	1020	1020	1020	1020	1020
Supplies	60	60	60	60	60	60
Insurance	300					
Custodial	120	120	120	120	120	120
Advertising	1048	1048	1048	748	748	748
Legal/Accounting	200	200	200	200	200	200
Communications	240	240	240	240	240	240
Royalty Payment	378	416	457	503	553	609
Co-op Ad Fund	126	139	152	168	184	203
Total Operating Expenditures	10082	9916	10064	9927	10106	10303
Pre-tax Profit	−5882	−5296	−4982	−4337	−3957	−3539
Income Taxes						
Net Income	−5882	−5296	−4982	−4337	−3957	−3539

68

Year One (*continued*)

7	8	9	10	11	12	Total	Percent
14881	16369	18006	19807	21787	23966	32366	1.00
7441	8185	9003	9903	10894	11983	16183	.50
7441	8185	9003	9903	10894	11983	16183	.50
5000	5000	5000	5000	5000	5000	10000	.31
750	750	750	750	750	750	1500	.05
1488	1637	1801	1981	2179	2397	3237	.10
1020	1020	1020	1020	1020	1020	2040	.06
60	60	60	60	60	60	120	.00
300						300	.01
120	120	120	120	120	120	240	.01
81	81	81	135	135	135	324	.01
200	200	200	200	200	200	400	.01
240	240	240	240	240	240	480	.01
670	737	810	891	980	1078	1456	.05
223	246	270	297	327	359	485	.02
10152	10090	10352	10694	11011	11359	20582	.64
−2711	−1905	−1349	−791	−117	624	−4399	
						0	
−2711	−1905	−1349	−791	−117	624	−4399	−.14

Franchisee Y projects the following net profits before taxes over the first six months:

	1	2	3	4	5	6
Net Profits	−12410	−4350	−972	1023	4730	7320

Y's cash flow for the first month is the same as his profit (minus 12,410). For the second month, his cash flow is minus 16,760. Here is how Y's cash flow develops for the six month period:

	1	2	3	4	5	6
Net Profits	−12410	−4350	−972	1023	4730	7320
Cash Flow	−12410	−16760	−17732	−16709	−11979	−4659

If Y continues to show a profit in later months, the cash flow deficit will eventually turn positive. Several important conclusions can be drawn from this analysis. For one thing, the maximum negative cash flow is a deficit of $17,732 at the end of month three. For another, the business cannot begin to pay back the investors until a positive cash flow develops.

The future backers of your business will use this analysis to determine how much short-term cash the business requires. They will also use it to figure when they will begin realizing a payback, and how much it will be.

Figure 8 shows an example proforma cash flow analysis for a typical franchise business.

PROFORMA FINANCIAL STATEMENT _____

A Financial Statement, sometimes referred to as a Balance Sheet, lists the assets and liabilities of the business, determining the net worth of the owner(s).

The assets of the business will include the following items:

Cash
Merchandise

Figure 8

Example of a Cash Flow Analysis

Cash Flow

Month	1	2	3	4	5	6
Month Start	0	−48875	−53984	−58632	−62772	−66353
Income	10200	11220	12342	13576	14934	16427
Expenditures	59905	17425	15901	16518	17197	17944
Month End	−49705	−55079	−57543	−61574	−65035	−67869

Month	7	8	9	10	11	12
Month Start	−67869	−70014	−71400	−71951	−71585	−70209
Income	18070	19877	21865	24051	26456	29102
Expenditures	18765	19668	20662	21756	22958	24281
Month End	−68564	−69805	−70198	−69656	−68087	−65388

Month	13	14	15	16	17	18
Month Start	−65388	−58857	−48824	−35071	17943	4045
Income	32012	35213	38735	42608	46869	51556
Expenditures	25481	25181	24981	25481	24881	24681
Month End	−58857	−48824	−35071	−17943	4045	30920

Month	19	20	21	22	23	24
Month Start	30920	36751	45933	57137	73039	93822
Income	32012	35213	38735	42608	46869	51556
Expenditures	26181	26031	27531	26706	26086	24681
Month End	36751	45933	57137	73039	93822	120697

Supplies
Amounts owed by customers
Land
Buildings
Furniture and fixtures

Equipment

Vehicles

Use the estimated or actual purchase price for each asset. The liabilities of the business include the following items:

Notes, loans, and other debts

Taxes payable

Interest expenses

Other liabilities such as accounts payable and unpaid wages are included in a conventional financial statement, but since yours is a projected statement, they may be omitted.

The bottom line of the Financial Statement reconciles the owner's equity (the difference between the assets and liabilities).

A sample financial statement is shown in Figure 9. As depicted in the example, the idea is to show the projected net worth of the business at the end of the three-year forecast period.

Figure 9

Example of a Proforma Financial Statement

PROFORMA FINANCIAL STATEMENT
(End of Year 3)

Assets

Current Assets

Cash on Hand	36,000	
Cash in Bank	48,400	
Accounts Receivable	9,200	
Interest Receivable	480	
Inventory	1,440	
Prepaid Expenses	5,400	
Total Current Assets	100,920	

Fixed Assets

Furnishings/Fixtures	13,000	
Vehicles/Equipment	170,000	
Total Fixed Assets	183,500	
Total Assets		283,920

Liabilities and Stockholder's Equity

Current Liabilities

Taxes Payable	2,400	
Debt Service	4,800	
Total Current Liabilities	7,200	
Long-term Debt	74,900	
Total Liabilities		82,100
Owner's Equity		201,820
Total Liabilities And Owner's Equity		283,920

OPERATING STATEMENT WORK SHEET

Year _____

Month	1	2	3	4	5
Net sales	$_____	$_____	$_____	$_____	$_____
Cost of goods	_____	_____	_____	_____	_____
Total Revenues	$_____	$_____	$_____	$_____	$_____
Salaries	$_____	$_____	$_____	$_____	$_____
Taxes/Benefits	_____	_____	_____	_____	_____
Commissions	_____	_____	_____	_____	_____
Space Lease	_____	_____	_____	_____	_____
Supplies	_____	_____	_____	_____	_____
Equipment	_____	_____	_____	_____	_____
Insurance	_____	_____	_____	_____	_____
Advertising	_____	_____	_____	_____	_____
Legal/Accounting	_____	_____	_____	_____	_____
Communications	_____	_____	_____	_____	_____
_____	_____	_____	_____	_____	_____
_____	_____	_____	_____	_____	_____
_____	_____	_____	_____	_____	_____
_____	_____	_____	_____	_____	_____
Royalty Payment	_____	_____	_____	_____	_____
Co-op Ad Fund	_____	_____	_____	_____	_____
Total Operating Expenditures	$_____	$_____	$_____	$_____	$_____
Pre-tax Profit	_____	_____	_____	_____	_____
Income Taxes	_____	_____	_____	_____	_____
Net Income	$_____	$_____	$_____	$_____	$_____

Year _____ (*continued*)

6	7	8	9	10	11	12
$_____	$_____	$_____	$_____	$_____	$_____	$_____
$_____	$_____	$_____	$_____	$_____	$_____	$_____
$_____	$_____	$_____	$_____	$_____	$_____	$_____
$_____	$_____	$_____	$_____	$_____	$_____	$_____
$_____	$_____	$_____	$_____	$_____	$_____	$_____

ANNUAL TOTALS

Year _____

	Total	Percent
Net Sales	$_____	1.00
Cost of Goods	_____	.___
Total Revenues	$_____	.___
Salaries	_____	.___
Taxes/Benefits	_____	.___
Commissions	_____	.___
Space Lease	_____	.___
Supplies	_____	.___
Equipment	_____	.___
Insurance	_____	.___
Advertising	_____	.___
Legal/Accounting	_____	.___
Communications	_____	.___
_____	_____	.___
_____	_____	.___
_____	_____	.___
Royalty Payment	_____	.___
Co-op Ad Fund	_____	.___
Total Operating Expenditures	$_____	.___
Pre-Tax Profit	_____	
Income Taxes	_____	
Net Income	$_____	

CASH FLOW ANALYSIS
WORK SHEET

Year _____

Month	1	2	3	4	5	6
Month Start	$____	$____	$____	$____	$____	$____
Income	____	____	____	____	____	____
Expenditures	____	____	____	____	____	____
Month End	$____	$____	$____	$____	$____	$____

Month	7	8	9	10	11	12
Month Start	$____	$____	$____	$____	$____	$____
Income	____	____	____	____	____	____
Expenditures	____	____	____	____	____	____
Month End	$____	$____	$____	$____	$____	$____

FINANCIAL STATEMENT
WORK SHEET

End of Year _____

Assets
Current Assets
    Cash on Hand $_____
    Cash in Bank   _____
    Accounts Receivable   _____
    Interest Receivable   _____
    Inventory   _____
    Prepaid Expenses   _____
    _____   _____
    _____   _____

Total Current Assets $_____
Fixed Assets
    Furnishings/Fixtures $_____
    Vehicles/Equipment   _____
    _____   _____
    _____   _____

Total Fixed Assets $_____
Total Assets $_____

Liabilities and Stockholder's Equity
Current Liabilities
    Taxes Payable $_____
    Debt Service   _____
    Accounts Payable   _____
    Royalties Payable   _____
Total Current Liabilities $_____
Long-Term Debt   _____
Total Liabilities $_____
Owners' Equity   _____
Total Liabilities and Owner's Equity $_____

5

Your Credentials

Two prospective franchisees, Richard C. and Robert T., live in different cities but have similar educational backgrounds and work histories. Each has held a position in management for just over seven years. During the same week, both were approved for franchises by the same franchising company, a well known hotel chain with a sterling track record.

Richard and Robert each assembled a financing proposal for his franchise business, and, having never met, both by coincidence sent their plans to the same investment group. This particular group specializes in hotels and has a favorable impression of that franchisor.

The two proposals had similar marketing plans and financial projections, in addition to the support of the same franchise organization. Yet the investment group funded Richard's proposal and turned down Robert's.

Why? The reason is not very mysterious. Robert's plan

identified only himself as the owner/operator of the business and, while mentioning other management positions by title, did not name any specific individuals. Richard's proposal described a highly qualified team of experienced hotel managers and advisers. Richard and Robert are real people, and their experience is a very real case in point.

All other considerations aside, to qualify for funding, a franchise must have at least two assets: a good franchisor and a good management team. In the mind of a financial backer, the *quality of the team* is the single most important factor influencing the decision to invest.

In many respects, the franchisor's credentials fight half the battle. Unlike other independent businesses, franchises are backed by the training, guidance, and know-how of an experienced team even before the first employee is hired. But the remaining 50 percent of the management qualifications is in your hands.

When a venture capitalist or banker looks at a business plan, he attempts to identify the following key management roles:

1. Chief executive
2. Marketing director
3. Financial director
4. Operations director

The persons filling these roles are carefully scrutinized with regard to their credentials. The roles they play are referred to as the "key result areas" of the business. The franchisor may supply training and guidance, but it is your own management team that will finally make the business successful.

Because your franchisor already has a track record, it is important to stress the qualifications of the franchisor's team as if its members were on your own payroll. In addition, you must be able to pencil in the names and backgrounds of qualified people to fill the business's internal key result areas.

Conduct a recruitment search, just as if you were actually hiring at this moment. Place a classified ad requesting résumés from qualified applicants. You might even go so far as to interview the leading candidates.

An executive recruiting agency will provide you with résumés of qualified applicants at no charge.

Having all the team members under contract is not necessary. Simply get their permission to pencil them into your business plan. You can always change your mind after the business is funded.

The management plan of your franchise financial proposal should consist of three parts:

1. Management résumé

2. Franchise résumé

3. Organization plan

MANAGEMENT RÉSUMÉ

The management résumé begins with your own personal credentials, as the chief executive officer of the proposed business. Provide a concise history of your personal background, specifically focusing on your vital data, health status, education, work experience, and professional or personal references.

Personal data

Describe your marital status, number of children, present and previous address, date and place of birth, and citizenship. Eliminate unnecessary details such as your height and weight. The important thing is to portray a sense of stability, direction, and responsibility.

Health status

Insert a statement asserting your good health and ability to successfully carry out the obligations and responsibilities of owning and developing a small business.

Education

List all relevant education and training, including secondary school, with institution name and city, and any college or trade education, designating the highest level of attendance. Also list any special seminars, certificates, or training programs attended, either on your own or as part of your employment with another company.

Work Experience

The first job you should list here (your present position) should be as chief operating executive of the new business. In succession, list each former job and employer, with a brief description of your responsibilities. Especially emphasize any experience that reflects on your ability to succeed at your proposed line of business. Provide the dates of employment by month and year.

Fill in any gaps in employment with a description of the appropriate activity—for instance, "Military Service, U.S. Marine Corps." If you have military experience as an officer or non-commissioned officer, be sure to emphasize that part of your work history.

Accounting for any gaps is crucial. If you have experienced a spell of unemployment, describe that period as a time when you were "self-employed" or acting as an "independent consultant." Leave no unexplained holes in your work history.

References

Provide three references who will vouch for your integrity and ability. A professional reference is generally preferable to a personal reference. List someone who can describe your on-the-job performance, rather than a friend unfamiliar with your past work habits.

Figure 10 shows a sample management résumé from a franchise financial proposal.

Besides yourself, include a profile of the people you have penciled in for the remaining roles on the management team—marketing, finance, and operations. Limit each profile to about one page, maximum of two.

Style

Most résumés are written in an outline style. The current trend is toward résumés that tell a story, using a narrative style.

Figure 10

MANAGEMENT RÉSUMÉ

Robert F. Ostlund President

Mr. Ostlund was born in Omaha, Nebraska on August 12, 1950. He is married, has two children, and is in excellent health.

He graduated from the University of Nebraska in 1972, with a major in mechanical engineering. He also attended the U.S. Navy Electronics School in Bethesda, Maryland.

From 1972 until 1978, Mr. Ostlund was a design engineer with Spectraphysics Corporation in San Jose, California, responsible for the design of instrumentation and processes used in the manufacture of biomedical equipment.

In 1978, he joined Varian Associates in Cupertino, California, as engineering manager. In March, November, 1986, he obtained the rights to open a Financial Future Counselors franchise in the San Jose market.

Mr. Ostlund possesses extensive experience in management, organizational planning, and project administration.

Regardless of the overall approach, it should be strictly to the point, avoiding first-person pronouns (I, me, my, we, us, our).

Use short, simple words which reduce reading time and effort ("try" instead of "endeavor", "get" rather than "obtain"). Active verbs paint a more powerful desription. Here are some examples:

Leadership verbs
administrated
directed
led
managed
supervised

Ingenuity verbs
composed
conceived

developed
founded
invented

Problem solver verbs
maximized
monitored
optimized
proved
scheduled
solved

Know-how verbs
built
designed
devised
engineered
generated
produced

Productivity verbs
accelerated
expanded
improved
increased
saved
streamlined

Accomplishment verbs
accomplished
delivered
expedited
performed
provided
trained

Conscientiousness verbs
began
established
launched
maintained
purchased
sold

Although the best possible profile may not get a business funded in the absence of bona fide qualifications, even the most qualified team has a slim likelihood of financial backing without a lucid and concise business plan. No matter how good your marketing and financial plans may look, a poorly presented profile of the management team is almost certain to be rejected.

PERSONAL FINANCIAL STATEMENT

If you have a positive net worth—that is, if the value of all your assets is greater than what you owe—include a personal financial statement after your profile.

State your assets and liabilities, and describe the type and amount of collateral you are willing to stake as a guarantee. It is not always necessary to have collateral to secure funding from an investment company, but an SBA-guaranteed loan may require some sort of collateral assurance. Often, the SBA will back business loans twice (or more) the amount of your available collateral.

Assets

Describe any property you own and list its current market value. Be sure to list any recreational or other liquid assets that beef up your net worth. List the amount in your checking and savings accounts, using the highest figure for the current month. Also include any stocks, bonds, precious metals, investments, or antiques, along with their current market value.

Liabilities

List the amount you owe on any unpaid notes, contracts, leases, residential loans, auto loans, etc. Include your estimated tax liability for the current year, unless, of course, you anticipate a refund.

Net Worth

Subtract your total liabilities from your total assets to determine your net worth. As a final step, add your net worth to your liabilities; the result should be the same as your total assets. Figure 11 shows an example of personal financial statement.

Notes to the Financial Statement

On a separate page titled "Notes," provide specific details about the data on your personal financial statement. Include the following information:

1. Documentation
2. Bank accounts
3. Collateral

Documentation

List the source of each asset and liability. For example, if you list real estate as an asset, describe the particular property or properties.

Bank Accounts

Give the bank name and account number for your checking, savings, credit card, or other accounts.

Figure 11

Example of a Personal Financial Statement
December 31, 1987

Assets

Residential Property	52,000	
Cash on Hand		
Checking Account	350	
Savings Account	2,400	
Vehicles and Equipment		
Delivery Van	5,200	
Boat and Motor	3,750	
Furnishings	2,200	
Total Assets		65,900

Liabilities

Loans Payable		
Mortgage	27,600	
Auto Loan	3,500	
Boat Loan	2,900	
Accounts Payable		
Mastercard	375	
Sears	425	
Taxes Payable	220	
Total Liabilities		35,020
Net Worth		30,880
Total Liabilities plus Net Worth		65,900

Collateral

Describe what type of collateral (if any) you intend to stake, and list its current market value.

The Advisory Team

Besides your internal management team, your business should have a team of qualified advisers in such specialized areas as finance and law. Your accountant and attorney are examples.

If possible, get a commitment from them to sit on your board of directors after the business is incorporated. Include that commitment in their individual profiles.

You, your advisors, or financial backers may decide on different board members later on. But including a list in your proposal indicates your thoroughness, as well as your dedication to the success of the business.

THE FRANCHISE RÉSUMÉ _____

Your franchisor's credentials are as important as your own. When a financier evaluates your financial proposal, the franchisor will be carefully scrutinized for his depth of experience, his demonstrated track record, and the benefits he brings to the operation.

Profiles of the franchisor's management team can be extracted from the Uniform Franchise Offering Circular, Section 2, Identity and Business Experience of Persons Affiliated with the Franchisor, includes brief resumes of the key team members.

Don't just photocopy the descriptions shown in the offering circular. Rewrite the profiles in a style that matches the other management résumés in your proposal.

THE ORGANIZATION PLAN _____

The final part of the management plan describes how you plan to organize and staff the operation. State the number of employees you can count on being with the business when you open the doors. If your staff will include members of your family, include them by name and job description. If your plan calls for hiring employees after you have received funding, list the number and provide a brief job description for each.

Decide whether your business will be operated as a sole proprietorship, a partnership, or a corporation. The simplest and least expensive way to operate a business is as a sole proprietorship; its debts are your own, and its income becomes your own personal taxable income. As a corporation, the business may receive less favorable tax treatment in some areas, but its liabilities are separate from your own. Shareholders are usually not liable for the debts of a corporation.

If you do decide to incorporate, include the names and addresses of all the shareholders, directors, and officers. If the business is run as a partnership, provide résumés and financial statements for each general partner.

Your financial backers may insist on a particular form of organization. For example, if a venture capital group decides to invest in your franchise, it will want to own shares in your corporation.

Include an organization chart showing each area of responsibility and the key team member who will head up the department. Figure 12 shows an example. Even though your franchise may be quite small, an organization chart lends credibility and substance to your proposal. It also demonstrates your ability to clearly define, organize, and manage the key result areas responsible for the success of the business.

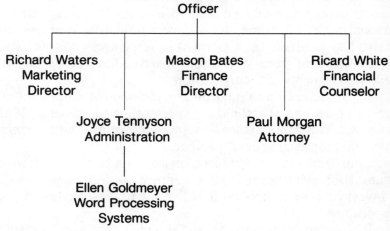

Figure 12

Example of an Organization Chart

FINANCIAL FUTURE COUNSELORS
Organization Chart

Robert F. Ostlund
Chief Executive
Officer

Richard Waters
Marketing
Director

Mason Bates
Finance
Director

Ricard White
Financial
Counselor

Joyce Tennyson
Administration

Paul Morgan
Attorney

Ellen Goldmeyer
Word Processing
Systems

SECTION
2

The
Sources

6

The
Payout

Perhaps the most obvious result of all your planning is a realistic snapshot of the true initial investment required to start your new business and sustain it until it begins to turn a profit. But why bother duplicating something your franchisor already gave you?

The initial investment breakdown in Section 7 of the Uniform Franchise Offering Circular, or UFOC, is based on rough estimates, usually in the form of high and low extremes. Although it may fulfill the regulatory requirements of the Federal Trade Commission (FTC), the breakdown is far from comprehensive.

The UFOC is not a free-form document. Its exact contents, ordering, and much of its wording are prescribed in detail by the FTC. Because the document is so similar to a securities prospectus, it is usually prepared by a consultant or attorney intimately familiar with the rules and regulations. Beyond the basic requirements, very little is added. The UFOC usually presents the minimum information required by government regulators, without much elaboration.

The estimated initial investment in your franchisor's UFOC may actually exclude some items which may be important to your survival, but which are not prescribed by the rules. Other estimates which may be included may not be meaningful in your case.

Working capital is a good example. The traditional meaning of the phrase "working capital" is a cash reserve sufficient to pay all the costs of staying in business until the company can stand on its own. Without this crucial reserve, a business is automatically doomed to failure. Yet the UFOC does not necessarily have to include an estimate of working capital at all. If the intial investment breakdown does include a working capital estimate, it is usually imprecise.

That is not to say that every franchisor's estimate of the franchisee's initial investment is wildly unreliable. Rather, the estimates are highly generalized and not tuned to your local economic conditions.

Your detailed financial plan tells you precisely how much cash infusion you need and when you need it. The amount is equal to the maximum value of negative cumulative cash flow in the worst-case projection at the end of any given month. Do not confuse this value with the net profit or loss for a specific month. Cumulative cash flow, as you recall, is the running total of all the previous month's profits and losses.

Here is an example. Franchisee Z's worst-case forecast looks like this:

	1	2	3	4	5	6
Profits	−38212	−9019	−5202	−1919	−480	24
Cash Flow	−38212	−47231	−52433	−54352	−54832	−54808

	7	8	9	10	11	12
Profits	3712	5660	7622	9750	12405	16412
Cash Flow	−51096	−45436	−37814	−28064	−15659	756

The end-of-year cumulative cash flow is the same as the total annual profit or loss. Z's franchise turns the corner in the sixth month, eeking out a slim profit of $24. In succeeding months, the negative cash trend is reversed by continuing profits. The maximum value of negative cumulative cash flow is $54,832 in month 5.

The common financing request is for double the amount, as insurance against unforeseen crises. Hence, in this example, Z would set out to obtain about $110,000 to start and sustain the business until it becomes profitable.

PRESENT VALUE

Knowing your capital requirements does not really tell you how much you will have to pay out in return. Obviously, no one will be interested in providing cash for your business without an additional return.

To estimate the payback, you must look at the business plan from the perspective of a banker or investor. These financial decision makers use various formulas to determine the true value of an investment. One is called *present value.*

The present value formula asks the question: what is a future payout worth in today's dollars? In other words, what is the correct amount to invest in order to realize a particular return? The formula for the present value of an investment may be reduced to a series of simple steps that can be handled with a calculator. But first, you must know two things: (1) the desired percentage return on the investment, and (2) the amount of the future payout. Following is the procedure:

1. Add 1 plus the percentage return.
2. Divide the payout amount by the total in step 1.
3. The result is the present value of the investment.

As an example, Investor Q is considering a proposal which will pay back $138,000. Q wants to realize a 15 percent return. The present value of the future payout is calculated as follows:

1. $1 + .15 = 1.15$

2. $\dfrac{138000}{1.15} = 120000$

3. Q should invest $120,000 today to receive a payout of $138,000 in the future.

Another way of looking at the rate of return is as the "cost" of money. In this example, the cost of money is 15 percent to pay out an $18,000 profit on a $120,000 investment.

Often, an investor wants to receive an ongoing payout over a period of time. To determine the present value in this situation requires a few additional steps. One more factor is necessary: the number of payout periods. The procedure for three equal payouts made over a three-year period is:

1. Add 1 plus the percentage return

2. Divide the payout amount by the total in step 1.

3. Raise the total in step 1 to the second power.

4. Divide the payout amount by the amount in step 3.

5. Raise the total in step 1 to the third power.

6. Divide the payout amount by the amount in step 5.

7. Add the results of steps 2, 4, and 6.

For example, Investor R wants to receive a $60,000 payout each year for a three-year period with a 20 percent rate of return. The present value of R's investment is calculated as follows:

1. $1 + .20 = 1.20$

2. $\dfrac{60000}{1.20} = 50000$

3. $1.20 \times 1.20 = 1.44$

4. $\dfrac{60000}{1.44} = 41667$

5. $1.20 \times 1.20 \times 1.20 = 1.728$

6. $\dfrac{60000}{1.728} = 34722$

7. $50000 + 41667 + 34722 = 126389$

R should invest $126,389 to realize three equal payments of
$60,000 over the next three years. As you can see in this exam-
ple, the present value of a future payout gets smaller and smaller
as the payout date is postponed. The first $60,000 payout costs
R $50,000; but when it is paid out three years from now, that
same $60,000 is only worth $34,722 today.

To determine the present value for two payouts over a two-
year period, just perform steps 1 through 4, adding the totals
from steps 2 and 4. For additional payout periods, simply raise
the exponent to the number of years; divide the payout amount
by the new fraction; and add the result to the running total.

For example, to determine the present value for four payouts over a four-year period, add the following steps:

8. Take the total in step 1 to the fourth power.

9. Divide the payout amount by the total in step 8.

10. Add the total in step 9 to the total in step 7.

If you prefer working with formulas, the present value formula looks like this:

$$PV = \frac{C_t}{\Sigma(1 + r_t)^t}$$

where PV = Present value
Σ = Sum of time period
C = Amount paid in year t
t = Time period
r = Rate of return in year t

In many investments, the payout amount will be different
in each period. For example, the investor might receive $10,000
in one year, $20,000 in the next, and $35,000 in the third. To
handle this scenario, substitute the applicable payout amount

in the appropriate step. The procedure for calculating the present value of three different payouts over a three-year period is:

1. Add 1 plus the percentage return.
2. Divide the first payout by the total in step 1.
3. Take the total in step 1 to the second power.
4. Divide the second payout by the total in step 1.
5. Take the total in step 1 to the third power.
6. Divide the third payout by the total in step 1.
7. Add the totals in steps 2, 4, and 6.

As an example, Investor S wants to receive payouts of $15,000, $25,000, and $35,000 over a three-year period, representing a 35 percent rate of return. The present value is calculated as follows:

1. $1 + .35 = 1.35$

2. $\dfrac{15000}{1.35} = 11111$

3. $1.35 \times 1.35 = 1.82$

4. $\dfrac{25000}{1.82} = 13736$

5. $1.35 \times 1.35 \times 1.35 = 2.46$

6. $\dfrac{35000}{2.46} = 14228$

7. $11111 + 13736 + 14228 = 39075$

S should invest $39,075 to receive the three payouts.

NET PRESENT VALUE _____

When a banker or investor is evaluating an investment, he calculates the *net present value,* not to be confused with ordinary present value just discussed. The net present value is a comparison of the terms of a proposed investment with the investor's minimum return. It determines whether the offer to invest is better or worse than the investor's expectations.

To calculate the net present value, you must know the amount of the initial investment, the proposed payout, and the minimum percentage return. Here is the procedure:

1. Determine the present value, based on the payout amount and the percentage return.

2. Subtract the initial investment from the present value.

3. The result is the net present value.

If the net present value is positive, the investment is a favorable proposition. If the value is negative, the proposal will most likely be rejected.

As an example, Investor T is evaluating a proposal to invest $120,000 to receive a payout of $162,500. T only considers investments which have at least a 30 percent return. The net present value is calculated thus:

1. (a) $1 + .30 = 1.30$

   (b) Present value $= \dfrac{162500}{1.30} = 125000$

2. $125000 - 120000 = 5000$

The net present value is positive, so the investment is a favorable proposition.

INTERNAL RATE OF RETURN

The net present value tells the investor only whether the proposal is good enough for his money. To determine the actual rate which the investment will produce, he must calculate the *internal rate of return.*

The procedure is as follows:

1. Divide the payout by the initial investment.

2. Subtract 1 from the amount in step one.

3. The result is the internal rate of return.

In the example of Investor T, investing $120,000 to receive a payback of $162,500, the internal rate of return would be calculated as follows:

1. $\dfrac{162500}{120000} = 1.354$

2. $1 - 1.354 = .354$

The internal rate of return for this investment is 35.4 percent. Therefore, the proposal exceeded T's minimum expectation of a 30 percent return.

The procedures in this chapter are simplified methods of calculating present value, net present value, and internal rate of return. The formulas become more complicated when different payouts and different rates of return are involved. The important thing is to keep it simple.

MAKING THE PAYOUT

Bear in mind you will not necessarily have to make the entire payout as a lump sum. Various ways of structuring the payout can meet the on-going needs of both the investor and your company.

The simplest form of payback is a conventional note or a bank loan, such as an SBA-guaranteed loan. With this method, you make monthly payments based on a stipulated interest rate, until both the loan and the rate are fully paid.

Another payback strategy is to issue stock in your corporation to the investor, guaranteeing to buy back all or part of the shares at an agreed price. In this manner, you effectively make just a single payout at the time of the buy-out.

Yet a third method is to issue stock and distribute profits in the form of dividends. In this way, you make the payout in quarterly, semi-annual, or annual portions.

These methods may even be combined in some fashion. For example, you might issue shares in your corporation, distribute dividends for five years, then buy back the stock at an agreed price.

A set of worksheets for determining present value, net present value, and internal rate of return is provided on the following pages. Use them to estimate how much you will have to pay out to receive the funding you need for your franchise. For a bank loan guaranteed by the SBA, use the current interest rate quoted by your bank as the rate of return. Bear in mind that an investment company or venture capitalist expects a return of 35 percent to 50 percent within three to five years.

Create a chart comparing the payout at various rates of return. Figure 13 shows an example. When you have determined the payout amounts, compare them with your financial forecasts. As you study the figures, try to answer the following questions.

- Which payout would be easiest to live with, based on your cash flow projections? What is the rate of return?
- Which payout and rate would be hardest to live with?
- Will there be enough positive cumulative cash flow over the next five years to make the payout?
- Which payout and rate of return would leave you with the most profits for yourself? Which would leave you with the least profits?
- Would it be better to pay out a single lump sum over one period, or to make several payouts?
- What would be the best way to pay back the investment: as profits distributed quarterly, semi-annually, or annually in the form of dividends? As a stock buy-back? Or as a gradual loan repayment?

Figure 13

Example of a Payout Comparison Chart

PAYOUT COMPARISON

Investment (Present Value)	Internal Rate of Return	No. of Payouts	Amount of each Payout	Total Payout
120000	35%	1	162000	162000
120000	50%	1	180000	180000
120000	100%	1	240000	240000
120000	200%	1	360000	360000
120000	300%	1	480000	480000
120000	50%	2	90000	180000
120000	100%	2	120000	240000
120000	200%	2	180000	360000
120000	300%	2	240000	480000
120000	50%	3	60000	180000
120000	100%	3	80000	240000
120000	200%	3	120000	360000
120000	300%	3	160000	480000
120000	100%	4	60000	240000
120000	200%	4	90000	360000
120000	300%	4	120000	480000
120000	100%	8	30000	240000
120000	300%	8	60000	480000
120000	100%	12	20000	240000
120000	300%	12	40000	480000

PRESENT VALUE OF AN INVESTMENT
WORK SHEET 1

Single Payout

1. Percentage rate of return, or interest: . _____

                                              +   1.000

2. Line 1 plus 1.000:   ___ . ___

3. Total payout: $_____

    Present Value = Line 3 divided by Line 1: $_____

WORK SHEET 1 *(Continued)*

Three Equal Payouts

1. Percentage rate of return, or interest: . _____

   + 1.000

2. Line 1 plus 1.000: ___ . ___

3. Amount of each payout: $_____

4. Line 3 divided by Line 2: $_____

5. Line 2 times Line 2 ___ . ___

6. Line 3 divided by Line 5: $_____

7. Line 2 times Line 5 ___ . ___

8. Line 3 divided by Line 7: $_____

   Present Value = Line 4 + Line 6 + Line 8: $_____

Three Unequal Payouts

1. Percentage rate of return, or interest: . _____

   + 1.000

2. Line 1 plus 1.000: ___ . ___

3. Amount of 1st payout: $_____

4. Line 3 divided by Line 2: $_____

5. Line 2 times Line 2 ___ . ___

6. Amount of 2nd payout: $_____

7. Line 6 divided by Line 5: $_____

8. Line 2 times Line 5 ___ . ___

9. Amount of 3rd payout: $_____

10. Line 9 divided by Line 8: $_____

   Present Value = Line 4 + Line 7 + Line 10: $_____

NET PRESENT VALUE

WORK SHEET 2

1. Rate of return, or interest: ___ . ___

      +   1.000

2. Line 1 plus 1.000: ___ . ___

3. Total payout: $_____

4. Present Value = Line 3 divided by Line 2: $_____

5. Initial investment: $_____

   Net Present Value = Line 4 less Line 5: $_____

INTERNAL RATE OF RETURN

WORK SHEET 3

Single Payout

1. Total payout: $_____

2. Initial investment: $_____

                                            1.000

3. Line 1 divided by Line 2:   ___.___

4. 1.000 less Line 3:   .___

    Internal Rate of Return = Line 4 × 100:   ___.___%

7

Putting
It All
Together

Having completed detailed plans for marketing, financing, and managing your business, you are at last prepared to assemble the Franchise Financial Plan for your venture, assuming, of course, you are still convinced the business is the right one for you. Although you embarked on these various planning processes with the intention of creating a definitive proposal, along the way you cannot have helped but gather a great deal of useful insight. You now know some important facts that previously were only suggested, hinted at, or estimated. Here are some of them:

Customer Knowledge

- Precisely who your customers are in your own trading area
- How many customers
- Where they are located
- The exact uses to which they will put your product
- What key decision makers are responsible for purchasing your product
- What factors influence their purchasing decisions
- Demographic traits of customers such as how old they are, and how much they earn

Competitor Knowledge

- Precisely who your competitors will be
- What products they carry
- What prices they charge
- How they advertise
- What percentage of the market they have captured
- Their strengths and weaknesses

Product Knowledge

- Precisely what products you will be selling
- What they can be used for
- Who needs or uses them
- How many to order and stock
- What price to sell them for

Financial Knowledge

- How many products you must sell each month
- What price ranges to emphasize

- What your month-to-month income will be
- What your variable expenses will be
- What your fixed expenses will be
- How much profit or loss you will make each month
- How much cash deficit or surplus will be available
- How much cash you will need to start the business
- How much capital you will need to pay the operating costs until the business can stand on its own

Organizational Knowledge

- Your own qualifications for this particular type of business
- Who will help you manage the business
- Their backgrounds and qualifications
- Who will advise you
- How many employees you will need
- Exactly when you will have to hire them
- How the business will be organized

Investment Knowledge

- Exactly how much cash you will have to obtain
- How much you should pay out in return
- The present value of the investment
- The net present value in relation to the expectations of various investors and financing sources
- The internal rate of return
- How to structure the payback

Before you began the Financial Plan, these facts were most likely only loosely or vaguely defined. It may well be that on detailed investigation, your contemplated franchise didn't turn out quite like you envisioned. On the other hand, it may be that the proposed business accurately meets your expectations— or even exceeds them. If that is the case, you are ready to put it all together.

ORGANIZATION

Assemble the venture proposal in the following order: the Business Statement first, the Marketing Plan second, then the Management Plan, and finally, the Financial Plan. The finishing touches are a one-page abstract and a table of contents.

The Abstract

The abstract, or overview, is a condensation of all the important conclusions drawn in the body of the proposal. It should consist of no more than a single page. When a potential investor sits down to review your proposal, he will begin by opening the cover and reading the abstract. Every financier's desk is stacked high with venture proposals. The initial screening involves no more than a quick glance at the abstract. Only 5 percent of the proposals in the stack will make it past this first stage. That select group will be determined on the basis of the abstract alone.

Clearly, this single-page introduction to the body of your proposal should not be taken lightly. But it is not the wording or style of the abstract that is important. The reviewer will look for certain key words and numbers. That is not to say that a clumsily worded abstract with numerous grammatical and spelling errors is not acceptable. At a minimum, the entire document must show a pristine regard for neatness, organization, and attention to detail.

When a venture proposal comes back from an investment group, someone has usually taken a red pencil to several items in the abstract. The items most commonly marked are:

- The amount of financing sought
- The product or service
- The customer

- The size of the market
- The profit projection

The abstract summarizes each of these key highlights of the proposal. If one of these items is missing, the reviewer may write the appropriate word in the margin with a question mark. Even though the information may be found in the body of the proposal, during this first stage of review the financier is only interested in the abstract. With hundreds of proposals to evaluate, he must rely on the abstract to tell him which few to read in depth.

1. **Amount of financing sought.**   The first sentence of the abstract should explain exactly how much cash you seek and how it will be used. The following is an example:

   Northeast Management Company is seeking $475,000 with which to develop a Traveler's Inn budget motel, under a franchise agreement with Traveler's Inns International, Inc.

2. **Business description.**   The next sentence should provide a concise description of the proposed business. The following is an example:

   The establishment will consist of 36 rooms with modern furnishings, offering comfortable lodging at competitive rates, in a location convenient for interstate travelers.

3. **The proposed use of the funds.**   In the same paragraph, describe how the financing will be used. The following sentence is an example:

   The investment will be applied to leasing and developing a site for the hotel, purchasing furnishings, and sustaining the operation until it begins to turn a profit.

4. **Location of the business.**   The next paragraph should describe the location. Use the address of the site you selected (or tentatively selected) during the planning process. Even though the location may be hypothetical at this stage, listing

its address lends substance to the abstract. The following is an example:

The motel will be located at 13128 N. Wood Canyon Blvd., one half block from the access to the North State Through-way.

5. **Description of the market.** Beginning a new paragraph, include a brief description of the market. If possible, include figures and amounts, to give the abstract a statistical tone. The following is an example:

Budget motels which target the low-end business and leisure traveler account for nearly 25 percent of all U.S. lodging expenditures, generating more than $1.2 billion annually.

6. **Description of the customer.** In the same paragraph, summarize your customer description. Stress demographics or details relevant to your particular location or trading area. If possible, include an estimate of the total number of potential customers for your business. The following is an example:

The primary customers for budget motels are sales representatives, other business travelers, and vacationing family units. According to Chamber of Commerce statistics, approximately 240,000 visitors to the North State area fall within this category each year.

7. **Profit projection.** In the final paragraph of the abstract, state the results of your three-year financial forecast. The following is an example:

Based on our three-year financial projection, the business will break even after 18 months, showing a pre-tax profit of $56,900 in the second year, increasing to $168,400 by the end of the third.

The completed abstract should be the very first page in your proposal. The second should be a table of contents.

THE TABLE OF CONTENTS

Besides directing the reader to the various sections of your proposal, the Table of Contents also serves as an outline. On first impression, it demonstrates your thoroughness, organizational skill, and attention to detail. Though similar to scores of other tables of contents, it can place your proposal in the upper class. An example table of contents based on the various sections described in this book is shown on page 118.

PRESENTATION

Your venture proposal must be neatly and accurately typed, then bound in a notebook or report folder. Remember, in the proposal business, first impressions count. How can you expect a venture capitalist or investment broker to fund a business from a ragged proposal full of mistyped words? Keep in mind that to the financial decision maker, your proposal is your business. A well organized, professional-looking proposal is critical. On the surface, it might seem little more than a stack of papers filled with words and numbers, but to the person who reviews it, the proposal is the business's only reality. Whoever looks at the plan will form his first and most lasting impression of how well your business will fare by how well your proposal looks.

Have the proposal typed or word-processed by a professional typist, so the entire document exudes businesslike organization and serious intent.

THE UNSUCCESSFUL PROPOSAL

A poorly presented proposal is almost certain to be rejected. The following list contains the most common faults for which venture proposals are routinely rejected during the initial review process:

1. *Sloppiness, lack of organization*

   Spelling or typing errors

   Poor design or format

   Unreadable or incomprehensible presentation

2. *Content problems*

   Failure to focus on specific qualifications of the management team

   Inaccuracies, omissions, or misrepresentations

   Irrelevant or superfluous information

3. *Nuisance value*

   Too long

   Too wordy or complex

The remainder of this chapter is devoted to a sample proposal which illustrates presentation, organization, and content. For the purposes of illustration, the example is intentionally abbreviated. A final proposal may actually contain between 50 and 100 pages.

A BUSINESS PROPOSAL
FOR
SHAPE UPS HEALTH CENTER
OF GREATER ELMWOOD

Prepared by:

Beverly Johnson
Shape Ups Health Center
2201 River Rd.
Elmwood, IL 55505
(800) 555-1212

TABLE OF CONTENTS

—————————— ABSTRACT ——————————

Shape Ups Health Center of Greater Elmwood, owned and operated by Beverly K. Johnson, is seeking $125,000 with which to develop a retail health assessment and exercise planning business, under a franchise agreement with Shape Ups International, Inc. The Shape Ups franchise is based on a unique system for evaluating individual health status and designing custom exercise routines with the aid of a microcomputer. The investment will be applied to obtaining commercial space for the business, purchasing exercise equipment, and sustaining the operation until it begins to turn a profit.

The principal business address will be at 534 Center Court, in the Fashion Central mall.

Public interest in health and fitness is greater today than at any previous time, generating more than $1.5 billion each year in the sale of health-related services and products. The typical customer is female, between 16 and 45 years of age, and from a middle to upper income household. According to Chamber of Commerce statistics, approximately 62,000 people in the Elmwood area fall into this category.

Based on our three-year financial projection, the business will break even in the fifth month, showing a pre-tax profit of $42,500 in the first year, increasing to $108,000 in the second year and $153,000 by the end of the third.

Business History

Shape Ups International was first organized as Shape Ups, Inc. in Los Angeles, California, in March, 1980. Based on a unique, computerized fitness counseling system, the company rapidly expanded from its original site into five retail fitness centers in the Los Angeles, Riverside, and San Diego areas. The company began franchising in December, 1982, establishing 81 franchises in 19 states.

Beverly Johnson first became involved in the health and fitness industry in June, 1982, as an exercise counselor for a major aerobic exercise spa based in Chicago. As she gained experience in the operation of a health spa, she noticed a pronounced need for an improved system of customizing exercise plans according to individual requirements. Researching the market, she found that all the fitness spas in the Elmwood area provided either group programs or unsupervised exercise, without a specific plan tailored to the physical needs of the enrollee.

In February, 1987, Ms. Johnson obtained franchise rights to establish a Shape Ups Health Center in the Elmwood market. In March, she conducted a survey of spa customers to determine the potential demand for this type of service. In a sampling of 100 enrollees in five different spas, 85% responded favorably, stating that they would enroll in such a service, if available.

In May, 1987, she organized Shape Ups Health Center of Greater Elmwood, obtained a license to conduct an exercise counseling business in the city of Elmwood, and selected a site for the operation.

Business Objectives

It is the objective of Shape Ups Health Center of Greater Elmwood to establish a health evaluation and fitness planning business at the Fashion Central mall in Elmwood, Illinois. The Grand Opening is tentatively planned for January, 1988.

The company intends to capture a 5% share of the health and fitness center market in the Elmwood area within two years.

Business Description

Enrollees in the Shape Ups program will receive a comprehensive health evaluation. Physical data about the individual will be entered into a microcomputer, along with the responses to a fitness questionnaire. Based on the results, the fitness counselor will recommend an individualized program consisting of an exercise plan, aerobic dancing, vitamins, and a health improvement diet program. The customer will receive a printout of the computer's results, plus a customized set of instructions outlining the recommended fitness program. The printout will include a schedule of ten weekly visits to the spa.

In addition, Shapemakers will sell vitamins and exercise books at retail prices.

Franchise Description

Shape Ups International is headquartered at 3001 North Central Avenue, Hollywood, California. The Shape Ups franchise includes comprehensive training in three weeks of intensive instruction at the Shape Ups Learning Center in Hollywood. In addition, a field trainer provides on-site training during the Grand Opening period.

Shape Ups franchisees also receive a detailed operations manual covering the use of the copyrighted computer program, client counseling techniques, exercise planning and administration, business operations, marketing, advertising, and personnel management.

Of the company's 81 franchisees, only one has closed since its opening, and another was re-purchased by the franchisor.

Market Analysis

According to the American Association of Sales and Marketing Executives, the health and fitness industry accounts for roughly $1.5 billion in annual sales. About $300 million is generated by exercise studios and health spas.

The fitness phenomenon is not confined to any geographic area, but is most widespread in major metropolitan and suburban areas.

Customer Analysis

Based on a demographic analysis of users of exercise spa services and products in the Elmwood area, the following customer profile was constructed:

Female	87%
Male	13
High school graduate	35
College graduate	45
Masters or higher	25
Single	34
Married	66

Household Income

$25,000 or less	20%
25,000 to 45,000	30
45,001 to 60,000	33
60,000 or more	17

Respondents were asked the following question: If a computerized health evaluation, exercise planning, and ten-week fitness improvement program were available for under $600, would you enroll?

Would enroll	85%
Would not enroll	10%
Undecided	5%

Based on this profile, the typical customer is female, college educated, and from a middle to upper income household. According to statistics published by the Greater Elmwood Chamber of Commerce, there are 62,000 individuals in this category in the Elmwood area.

Top Health Services Markets

Rank	Market	Sales (millions)
1	Los Angeles	3.20
2	New York	3.04
3	Chicago	2.39
4	Washington, DC	1.99
5	Philadelphia	1.90
6	Houston	1.70
7	San Francisco	1.57
8	Dallas	1.49
9	Boston	1.27
10	St. Louis	1.18
11	Cleveland	.94
12	Detroit	.83
13	Nassau, NY	.81
14	Pittsburgh	.80
15	Baltimore	.78
16	San Diego	.75
17	Anaheim	.75
18	Tampa	.69
19	Seattle	.68
20	Phoenix	.66
21	Kansas City	.63
22	Newark	.62
23	Atlanta	.62
24	Minneapolis	.61
25	Miami	.56
26	Cincinatti	.53
27	New Orleans	.47
28	Denver	.46
29	Indianapolis	.46

30	San Jose	.45
31	Milwaukee	.44
32	Buffalo	.44
33	Columbus	.41
34	Honolulu	.41
35	Hartford, CT	.38
36	Louisville	.38
37	Riverside, CA	.38
38	Norfolk, VA	.37
39	Oklahoma City	.36
40	Birmingham	.36
41	Rochester, NY	.35
42	Richmond	.34
43	Salt Lake City	.34
44	Ft. Lauderdale	.32
45	Portland	.31
46	Tulsa	.31
47	Memphis	.31
48	Omaha	.31
49	Gary, IN	.30
50	Nashville	.30

Product/Service Mix

Shape Ups health centers offer the following products and services:

1. Basic Service

Computer-aided health evaluation and fitness planning service, tailored to the specific exercise needs of the individual.

2. Annual Membership

In addition to the Basic Service, clients may opt for annual membership, entitling them to utilize Shape Ups facilities and equipment up to ten hours per week during the term of membership.

3. Vitamins and health supplements

4. Health-related and fitness-related books

5. Videotapes on health-related subjects

Advertising Plan

Four promotional tools will be used to market the service:

1. Group presentations

Shapemakers will conduct group seminars, free to the public, at which the program will be outlined and attendees will be allowed to use the facilities of the spa for one hour without charge. Clubs, businesses, and members of the media will be invited to the seminars.

2. Newspaper

A display ad will run twice each week in The Elmwood Chronicle, each Tuesday and Sunday. The Tuesday ad will promote the facilities, and the Sunday ad will invite the public to attend one of the biweekly seminars.

3. Direct Mail

An envelope-size flier will be printed for use in a direct-mail campaign to residents of upper-income neighborhoods in the Elmwood vicinity, and to secretarial personnel in local businesses.

4. Yellow Pages

A prominent display ad will be purchased in the Yellow Pages.
     The costs of developing and administering these programs are reflected in the Financial Plan.

Competition Analysis

Classic Fitness Center

This firm is owned by Frank Justin, and has been operating in the Elmwood area since 1982. Classic Fitness is a standard exercise equipment center for weight loss and strength development, with no direct supervision or individual planning. The company offers a ten-week enrollment for $695.

Strengths: An established business with good name recognition and more than 300 enrollees. Well equipped with a capable staff of seven counselors.

Weaknesses: Classic Fitness does not offer individualized planning or health assessment. Once the customer is enrolled, there is little or no individual counseling or followup.

MANAGEMENT PLAN

Managment Résumé

Beverly Johnson
Owner/operator

Beverly Johnson was born in Davenport, Illinois on June 22, 1955. She is a U.S. citizen, married, and has a daughter, age five. Her health is excellent.

Ms. Johnson graduated from Pine Grove Business College in June, 1977. She completed a training program in exercise counseling conducted by Fitness Professionals, Inc. of Chicago in 1981.

Ms. Johnson has been the owner and operator of Shape Ups Health Center of Greater Elmwood since its organization in February, 1987.

Previously, she was the manager of Classic Fitness Center in Elmwood, Illinois from July, 1983, until January, 1987.

Erica Sandel
Marketing Director

Ms. Erica Sandel is a knowledgeable spa administrator with over ten years' experience in managing two different fitness centers. As director of Shapemaker Spas in Lakeside, Illinois from August, 1981 until February, 1987, she increased annual sales from $40,000 to over $250,000.

She was previously administrator of New Wave Aerobicise Center in Des Moines, Iowa, from July, 1974 until August, 1981.

Thomas Rudd
Director of Operations

Mr. Rudd graduated from University of Chicago with a major in physical education.

From July, 1983 until January, 1987, he was employed by Classic Fitness Center as head fitness counselor.

Mr. Rudd is thoroughly knowledgeable in all aspects of fitness counseling, exercise equipment, and program administration.

David Sinclair
Financial Advisor

The business's books will be kept by the accounting firm of David Sinclair, CPA. Mr. Sinclair has a master's degree in finance from the University of Indiana, and a bachelor's in business administration from the University of California at Los Angeles.

He has been a Certified Public Accountant since August, 1979, handling the accounting and bookkeeping responsibilities for more than 50 clients over the last eight years.

His previous clients include three exercise businesses similar to Shape Ups Health Center.

Personal Financial Statement
of
Beverly K. Johnson

Assets

Cash on Hand		
Checking account	$ 300	
Savings account	1,200	
Vehicles & equipment		
Auto	5,400	
Exercise equipment	800	
Furnishings	1,800	
TOTAL ASSETS		$9,500

Liabilities

Loans payable		
Auto loan	$2,600	
Accounts payable		
Visa	200	
J C Penney	100	
TOTAL LIABILITIES	$2,900	
NET WORTH	$6,600	
TOTAL LIABILITIES PLUS NET WORTH		$9,500

Organization and Staff

The operation requires the following minimum staff:

1. General manager and fitness counselor

Fulltime. Responsible for supervision of all employees and administration of the health assessment program. Designs individualized exercise plans based on computer results.

2. Office manager

Fulltime. Responsible for marketing and recruiting of enrollees. Delivers group presentations to clubs, businesses, and local media. Enrolls new customers and monitors payments.

3. Exercise counselor

Fulltime. Responsible for supervising individual exercise programs and maintaining equipment in good working condition.

4. Receptionist Fulltime.

Responsible for spa reception, filing, telephone answering, typing, and general clerical assistance.

The following matrix shows the organization of the business according to specific responsibility.

	Administration	Marketing and Sales	Health Evaluation	Exercise Counsel
B. Johnson	X	X	X	X
E. Sandel	X	X		
T. Rudd			X	X

Financial Forecast
Proforma Operating Statement

Year One

Month	1	2	3	4	5	6
Net Sales	3120	3744	4493	5391	6470	7764
Cost of Goods	60	72	86	104	124	149
Total Revenues	3060	3672	4406	5288	6345	7614
Salaries	3600	3600	3600	3600	3600	3600
Taxes/Benefits	540	540	540	540	540	540
Commissions	468	562	674	809	970	1165
Space Lease	900	900	900	900	900	900
Supplies	62	75	90	108	129	155
Equipment	37500					
Insurance	300					
Maintenance	62	75	90	108	129	155
Advertising	1500	1500	1500	1500	1500	1500
Legal/Accounting	150	150	150	150	150	150
Communications	300	300	300	300	300	300
Royalty Payment	153	184	220	264	317	381
Co-op Ad Fund	61	73	88	106	127	152
Total Operating Expenses	45597	7958	8152	8384	8663	8998
Pre-tax Profit	−42537	−4286	−3746	−3097	−2318	−1384
Income taxes						
Net Income	−42537	−4286	−3746	−3097	−2318	−1384

Year One (*continued*)

7	8	9	10	11	12	Total	Percent
9316	11180	13415	16099	19318	23182	123491	1.00
179	215	258	310	372	446	2375	.02
9137	10965	13157	15789	18947	22736	121116	.98
3600	3600	3600	3600	3600	3600	43200	.35
540	540	540	540	540	540	6480	.05
1397	1677	2012	2415	2898	3477	18524	.15
900	900	900	900	900	900	10800	.09
186	224	268	322	386	464	2470	.02
300						600	.01
186	224	268	322	386	464	2470	.02
1500	1500	1500	1500	1500	1500	18000	.15
150	150	150	150	150	150	1800	.01
300	300	300	300	300	300	3600	.03
457	548	658	789	947	1137	6056	.05
183	219	263	316	379	455	2422	.02
9700	9882	10460	11154	11987	12986	153921	1.25
−563	1083	2697	4635	6960	9750	−32805	
						0	
−563	1083	2697	4635	6960	9750	−32805	

Financial Forecast Proforma Operating Statement *(Continued)*

Year Two

Month	13	14	15	16	17	18
Net Sales	23646	24119	24601	25093	25595	26107
Cost of Goods	455	464	473	483	492	502
Total Revenues	23191	23655	24128	24610	25103	25605
Salaries	3960	3960	3960	3960	3960	3960
Taxes/Benefits	594	594	594	594	594	594
Commissions	3547	3618	3690	3764	3839	3916
Space Lease	900	900	900	900	900	900
Supplies	473	482	492	502	512	522
Equipment						
Insurance	300					
Maintenance	473	482	492	502	512	522
Advertising	1500	1500	1500	1500	1500	1500
Legal/Accounting	150	150	150	150	150	150
Communications	300	300	300	300	300	300
Royalty Payments	1160	1183	1206	1231	1255	1280
Co-op Ad Fund	464	473	483	492	502	512
Total Operating Expenditures	13820	13642	13767	13894	14024	14157
Pre-tax Profit	9371	10012	10361	10716	11078	11448
Income Taxes			4144	4286	4431	4579
Net Income	9371	10012	6216	6430	6647	6869
Cumulative Cash Flow	−29041	−19029	−12812	−6383	264	7133

Year Two *(Continued)*

19	20	21	22	23	24	Total	Percent
26629	27161	27705	28259	28824	29400	317137	1.00
512	522	533	543	554	565	6099	.02
26117	26639	27172	27715	28270	28835	311039	.98
3960	3960	3960	3960	3960	3960	47520	.15
594	594	594	594	594	594	7128	.02
3994	4074	4156	4239	4324	4410	47571	.15
900	900	900	900	900	900	10800	.03
533	543	554	565	576	588	6343	.02
3000							
300						600	.01
533	543	554	565	576	588	6343	.02
1500	1500	1500	1500	1500	1500	18000	.06
150	150	150	150	150	150	1800	.01
300	300	300	300	300	300	3600	.01
1306	1332	1359	1386	1413	1442	15552	.05
522	533	543	554	565	577	6221	.02
17592	14429	14570	14713	14859	15009	174477	.55
8525	12210	12602	13002	13410	13826	136562	
3410	4884	5041	5201	5364	5531	46871	
5115	7326	7561	7801	8046	8296	89690	.28
12248	19574	27135	34936	42983	51278		

Financial Forecast Proforma Operating Statement *(Continued)*

Year Three

Month	25	26	27	28	29	30
Net Sales	29400	29400	29400	29400	29400	29400
Cost of Goods	565	565	565	565	565	565
Total Revenues	28835	28835	28835	28835	28835	28835
Salaries	5990	5990	5990	5990	5990	5990
Taxes/Benefits	899	899	899	899	899	899
Commissions	4410	4410	4410	4410	4410	4410
Space Lease	900	900	900	900	900	900
Supplies	588	588	588	588	588	588
Equipment	4500					
Insurance	300					
Maintenance	588	588	588	588	588	588
Advertising	1500	1500	1500	1500	1500	1500
Legal/Accounting	150	150	150	150	150	150
Communications	300	300	300	300	300	300
Royalty Payments	1442	1442	1442	1442	1442	1442
Co-op Ad Fund	577	577	577	577	577	577
Total Operating Expenditures	22143	17343	17343	17343	17343	17343
Pre-tax Profit	6692	11492	11492	11492	11492	11492
Income Taxes			4597	4597	4597	4597
Net Income	6692	11492	6895	6895	6895	6895
Cumulative Cash Flow	−31720	−20229	−13334	−6439	456	7351

31	32	33	34	35	36	Total	Percent
29400	29400	29400	29400	29400	29400	352800	1.00
565	565	565	565	565	565	6785	.02
28835	28835	28835	28835	28835	28835	346015	.98
5990	5990	5990	5990	5990	5990	71880	.20
899	899	899	899	899	899	10782	.03
4410	4410	4410	4410	4410	4410	52920	.15
900	900	900	900	900	900	10800	.03
588	588	588	588	588	588	7056	.02
3000							
300						600	.01
588	588	588	588	588	588	7056	.02
1500	1500	1500	1500	1500	1500	18000	.05
150	150	150	150	150	150	1800	.01
300	300	300	300	300	300	3600	.01
1442	1442	1442	1442	1442	1442	17301	.05
577	577	577	577	577	577	6920	.02
20643	17343	17343	17343	17343	17343	216215	.61
8192	11492	11492	11492	11492	11492	129800	
3277	4597	4597	4597	4597	4597	44647	
4915	6895	6895	6895	6895	6895	85154	.24
2266	19161	26056	32952	39847	46742		

Cash Flow Analysis

Month	1	2	3	4	5	6
Month Start	0	−42537	−46823	−50569	−53666	−5598⁴
Total Revenues	3060	3672	4406	5288	6345	761⁴
Expenditures	45597	7958	8152	8384	8663	899⁸
Month End	−42537	−46823	−50569	−53666	−55984	−5736⁸

Month	7	8	9	10	11	12
Month Start	−57368	−57930	−56848	−54150	−49515	−4255⁵
Total Revenues	9137	10965	13157	15789	18947	2273⁰
Expenditures	9700	9882	10460	11154	11987	1298⁰
Month End	−57930	−56848	−54150	−49515	−42555	−3280⁵

Month	13	14	15	16	17	18
Month Start	−32805	−23434	−13422	−3061	7655	1873³
Income	23191	23655	24128	24610	25103	2560⁵
Expenditures	13820	13642	13767	13894	14024	1415⁷
Month End	−23434	−13422	−3061	7655	18733	3018

Month	19	20	21	22	23	24
Month Start	30181	38706	50916	63518	76520	8993⁰
Income	26117	26639	27172	27715	28270	2883⁵
Expenditures	17592	14429	14570	14713	14859	1500⁹
Month End	38706	50916	63518	76520	89930	10375⁷

Month	25	26	27	28	29	30
Month Start	103757	110449	121940	133432	144924	15641⁵
Income	28835	28835	28835	28835	28835	2883⁵
Expenditures	22143	17343	17343	17343	17343	1734³
Month End	110449	121940	133432	144924	156415	16790⁷

Month	31	32	33	34	35	36
Month Start	167907	176099	187591	199082	210574	22206⁰
Income	28835	28835	28835	28835	28835	2883⁵
Expenditures	20643	17343	17343	17343	17343	1734³
Month End	176099	187591	199082	210574	222066	23355⁷

8

Making the Rounds

Now that you have a complete, professional-looking Financial Plan for your franchise business, what do you do with it? You know generally what you want: to raise the cash outlay required to start, develop, and open the new business. Ideally, you would like to leverage the business in such a way as to avoid having to invest any personal funds at all. But if possible you would also avoid the burden of interest payments—the debt service—that often saddles a new business for years.

The possibility does exist to avoid debt service when you use other people's money to finance a new business. However, it might not be desirable, depending on your individual circumstances.

For example, consider that you succeed in convincing a venture capital manager to invest seed money in your idea. For the venture capitalist, the investment is a high-risk proposition. In return, he will want a guarantee that (a) you will pay out a proportionately large return in rather short order; or (b) you will back your promise to pay with 50 percent or more ownership in the business.

In other words, if you default on your ability to compensate the venture capitalist, he will have the option to swoop in and take over the entire operation for virtually nothing. Of course, this risk-payout relationship works both ways. True, the venture capitalist is taking a great risk in funding your idea, but on the other hand, you are staking your owner's share of the business. If the business succeeds and the payout is satisfactory to all concerned, then no one is likely to complain.

Once the capital group is repaid, obligation is dissolved. Venture capitalists expect a high return (50–100 percent within five years). But compare this percentage with a lengthy, strung-out debt service—like a conventional bank loan—and you might find the venture capitalist's money to be a bargain.

At the opposite end of the spectrum is the SBA-guaranteed loan; to qualify, you must be turned down by at least three conventional lending institutions. The loan is actually extended by a local bank in your trading area, but the SBA guarantees to fulfill your obligations if you should happen to default.

SBICs AND MESBICs

A particularly attractive source of funding is the licensed Small Business Investment Company (SBIC). This operation is actually an independent venture capital group licensed by the government to lend funds to small business startups. An offshoot of this entity is the Minority Enterprise Small Business Investment Company, or MESBIC (high on the government's list of business priorities, for obvious political reasons).

To illustrate a MESBIC investment, let's look at a case history.

The person I referred to earlier in the book as "George" is a real individual. Of course, George is a pseudonym used to avoid giving free publicity to any particular person or business.

George, as you recall, wanted to be his own boss. He knew there was money available for new business startups, but when he contacted the nearest SBIC, he found that most of the funds available were earmarked for minority enterprises under MESBIC. Remember that George had already been turned down by several banks. Unfortunately for him, George was not a member of any officially recognized minority group. But on examination, he discovered that under MESBIC guidelines women are considered a minority group in the business world.

So George structured his business plan with his wife as co-owner of the business—in fact, the owner of 51 percent of the outstanding shares—and thereby qualified for the funds he needed to start his business.

Of course, if you are a member of an officially recognized minority, you already meet the basic test.

To obtain a list of SBICs, write to the National Association of Small Business Investment Companies, 512 Washington Bldg, Washington, DC 20005, (202) 638-3411.

The association can supply you with names, addresses, telephone numbers, and persons to contact in your locality. Besides SBA-type business loans, many of these firms manage venture capital pools earmarked for small business startups in a diversity of fields.

Whereas SBICs are licensed by the Small Business Administration, a MESBIC may also be subsidized by the Minority Business Development Agency. To locate a MESBIC in your area, contact your local SBA office.

SBA GUARANTEED LOANS

Entrepreneurs have long regarded the Small Business Administration as a kind of economic equalizer, keeping afloat the entrepreneurial spirit that forged America's greatness. But in recent years, that ideal has been repeatedly challenged by politicians and special-interest groups, primarily big business proponents who argue that America already has "too many small businesses."

In 1984, the U.S. Office of Management and Budget

launched an aggressive campaign to shut down the SBA, citing its $9.8 billion loan portfolio and its ungainly 19 percent default rate. Though the campaign was spearheaded by the Budget Office, it was inspired by lobbying efforts of large commercial banks, who have always viewed the SBA as a competitor in the marketplace for small business loans. Yet, fewer than 0.2 percent of the nation's business owners actually are served by the SBA. Moreover, without SBA assistance, most of these would not be in business at all, deteriorating—rather than bolstering—the market for commercial loans. Apparently, the banking lobbyists simply overlooked the fact that once a business becomes successful and no longer requires SBA assistance, it is a ripe candidate for a commercial loan from a conventional lending establishment.

In part for these reasons, the Budget Office was unsuccessful in its attempts to close the SBA and sell off its loan portfolio at a discount. Fortunately, the SBA is one of Congress's darlings, one of the few federal assistance programs that directly cultivates new business entities. Few legislators are willing to vote for abolishing the SBA and explaining to their constituents why they helped pound a nail in the coffin of the American dream.

Nonetheless, SBA funding was dramatically reduced in 1985 and will continue to be austere as long as the federal deficit is astronomical. When and if U.S. administrations manage to achieve significant reductions in the national debt—presumably within the next two or three years—funds for small business assistance will undoubtedly begin flowing into the economy with renewed vigor, whether through the SBA or through some counterpart entity.

Even in today's atmosphere of nonmilitary austerity, SBA funds are sporadically available. But they are invariably committed almost as soon as they are received, and timing is crucial to obtaining even a penny of the money earmarked for American entrepreneurs like yourself.

To secure financial assistance through the SBA, you must first be turned down by at least three banks. If you are interested in SBA assistance, get an appointment with your local SBA loan officer to discuss your Business Financial Plan. He will tell you the procedures for submitting your application and even direct you to specific banks to get the declinal process over with. In many instances, the officer will help streamline the approval process. SBIC, MESBIC, SBA, and venture capital financing is a time consuming process and may well require from three to six months.

If you want to read up on the SBA and the different types of loan programs available, write to the Small Business Administration, Washington, DC 20416. Request the publication entitled "SBA Business Loans" (Publication No. OPI 15).

VENTURE CAPITALISTS

Each year, more than 7,000 new businesses are financed by venture capitalists. The total amount of capital represented by these investments exceeds $12 billion. Besides the established venture capital investment groups, thousands of small, independent investors look for "little businesses" to latch onto.

Initial venture capital investments fall into two general categories: seed capital and start-up capital.

Seed Capital

Seed money is an investment in an idea. It is used to fund the development and elaboration of the idea itself, rather than the working capital required to sustain a full-fledged operation. Consequently, the investment is much riskier from the venture capitalist's point of view. At this level of funding, you should expect to sacrifice a proportionately larger stake in the future business.

Startup Capital

Startup money is an investment in a new business with an existing business plan and management team already in place. It is the small time operator's most viable source of venture funding. For the venture capitalist, the risk is slighter yet the payoff is potentially high. The investment is used to kick off the marketing program that will transform the entrepreneur's idea into a cash-producing business.

To attract start-up money, you will need a good business plan and an able management team, not necessarily a fulltime staff of Harvard MBAs, but a line-up of experienced specialists willing to put their names in your business plan. Get the person you can find to fill each niche. Ink their salary requirements into your business plan; you are under no obligation unless and until you actually receive funding.

The next step is contacting the right venture capital group. These firms tend to specialize in certain types of businesses. To obtain current lists of active venture capitalists, investment partnerships, and licensed SBICs, contact the following firm:

Capital Publishing Corporation
10 S. LaSalle St.
Chicago, IL 60603
(312) 641-0922

This company publishes a list of venture capital sources, listing areas of interest, qualification criteria, and contact names and addresses.

John Wiley & Sons also publishes an annual directory titled *Who's Who in Venture Capital* by A. David Silver. You can obtain a copy from your local book dealer; if you don't find it on the shelf, ask the store manager to order a copy for you.

INDEPENDENT INVESTORS

Besides venture capital groups, numerous small-time independent investors are constantly on the prowl for ripe start-up opportunities. Most are retired or semi-retired executives or military officers with money to invest. Many long to participate as an active partner and can fill one of the vital roles required to achieve success, for example, as finance director or marketing director.

Like a venture capitalist, the independent investor is looking for an attractive payoff and an honest share of ownership. However, whereas a venture capitalist would rather not own more than 40 percent of your business, most independents will ask for half.

The two best sources for locating independent investors are small business brokers and the classified section of your daily metropolitan newspaper. Take your finished plan to a business broker (not a real estate or stock broker); he may already know a client looking for just such an opportunity.

Advertising for a partner in the classified section of your daily newspaper is legal in most states. However, it may not be permissible simply to advertise for money. It is absolutely illegal to offer to sell securities, such as stock in your corporation. The best advice is to advertise for a general manager with partnership possibilities. A sample ad might read:

GENERAL MANAGER/PARTNER.
Progressive, growth-oriented franchise in a dynamic growth industry seeks active partner for investment and participation.

As you receive résumés, add the name, address, and phone number of each respondent to a list of prospective investors.

SUBMITTING THE PROPOSAL

Before you shop with proposal, compile a list of investment companies, business brokers, and lending institutions. Submit the proposal to no more than three sources at a time.

Select three potential financing sources from the list. Unless you are specifically going after only one type of funding, for example, a guaranteed business loan, select each source from a different category: one SBIC, one bank or finance company participating in the SBA loan program, and one venture capital group or independent investor.

Call the contact person or investor and explain that you would like to submit a venture proposal for consideration. You will be asked to briefly explain the business concept, as well as the amount of money you seek. Refer to the abstract to make an intelligent reply, without reading the answers word for word.

If the investor is not interested in your particular business or industry, or deems the amount too trivial, you will at least succeed in avoiding the cost and time of a pointless submission.

If, on the other hand, you are invited to submit your proposal, you have helped establish rapport by attaching a human voice to your meticulously typed document.

Although "blind" submissions to a scattering of addresses do not usually produce concrete results, some investment groups do not have the time or personnel to screen prospects by phone, and prefer that proposals be sent without preliminary contact.

Whether you mail your proposal as a result of a phone conversation with a potential investor, or whether you send it anonymously, include a copy of sections 1–20 of your franchisor's Uniform Franchise Offering Circular. It is not necessary or advisable to include a copy of the franchise agreement or the audited financial statements of the franchisor. In addition to the UFOC, include a cover letter with every submission.

The Cover Letter

The cover letter represents an opportunity to personalize your proposal and express your qualifications in a subjective light. Your cover letter should include some of the key highlights contained in the abstract, but without answering all the crucial questions.

The reviewer will read the abstract to form an initial evaluation, but first, your cover letter to decide whether or not to spend valuable time reading the abstract. Thus, the objective of the cover letter is to "hook" the reviewer into opening the proposal, not to duplicate the information contained in the abstract.

Say just enough to whet the investor's appetite, but not enough to enable him to form a judgment. Leave an element of mystery, to entice him to delve further into your proposal.

For the purposes of submitting your venture proposal, there are two types of cover letters: personal and broadcast.

The personal cover letter is written in response to a specific invitation, usually as the result of an initial phone conversation. Its advantage lies in its potential to create a more personal image for the business plan.

The broadcast letter is written in general terms for distribution to multiple prospective investors. It may even be sent without a proposal.

Here are some guidelines to follow:

1. Limit the cover letter to two to four paragraphs.

2. Use a standard business letter format.

3. Personalize the salutation. Invest the time and effort to identify the personnel director's name. Avoid using "To whom it may concern" or a similarly impersonal greeting.

4. At the end of the letter, immediately following the text, use a complimentary close, such as "Best regards" or "Very truly yours."

The message portion of the cover letter is divided into three basic parts:

1. **Introduction.**   State specifically why you are writing.

2. **Body.**   Briefly capsulize the business, franchise, product, and market. Avoid specifying how much cash you are looking for, or what your projected profits will be.

   The cover letter provides an opportunity to amplify or expand on any special accomplishments only lightly mentioned in the proposal. It also provides a forum for describing special characteristics not normally included in the résumé, such as personal creativity, problem solving ability, communication or administrative skills.

3. **Conclusion.**   Use a call to action to motivate a specific response. For instance, you might promise to call to discuss the proposal, or suggest a time when you might be called.

   An example of a personal cover letter is shown in Figure 14. A sample broadcast letter is shown in Figure 15.

THE INTERVIEW

If your proposal appears promising to a potential financing source, you will be invited for a personal interview. The interview is a preplanned conversation with a structure and a purpose. It is both information-giving and information-receiving.

Figure 14

Sample Personal Cover Letter

July 6, 1987

David Cole
American Builders of Eugene
89019 Mercantile Drive
Eugene, Oregon 59019

Mr. Steven Hurlbut
Capital Associates
2021 N. Cheshire Blvd.
Woodmont, California 90002

Dear Mr. Hurlbut,

Enclosed please find our business proposal for an American Builders franchise in the Eugene, Oregon market. As you may be aware, American Builders is a well established franchisor in the construction and remodeling industry. Franchisees receive comprehensive training, national advertising, volume discounts on materials and supplies, and the backing of an industry leader.

Our management team ideally fulfills the requirements of both the franchise and our venture plan. The proposal contains a detailed market analysis, financial projections, management plan, and our personal credentials.

I will be available during the week of July 21 to answer any questions you may have or to schedule an appointment. Thank you for your time and consideration.

Best regards,

David C. Cole
President

Figure 15

Sample Broadcast Cover Letter

July 12, 1987

David Cole
American Builders of Eugene
89019 Mercantile Drive
Eugene, Oregon 59019

All Century Venture Corporation
P.O. Box 107
Chicago, Illinois 50510

Gentlemen:

The enclosed proposal is submitted in response to your advertisement for new ventures in the June 21 edition of the Wall Street Journal. The proposal contains a detailed market analysis, financial projections, management plan, and our personal credentials.

I will be available during the week of July 28 to answer any questions you may have. Thank you for your time and consideration.

Best regards,

David C. Cole
President

For the investor or lender, the interview is an important opportunity to explore your qualifications and resolve any questions that may have arisen concerning your business plan. It is also an opportunity for the investor to sell you on his firm.

When you arrive at the interview, be prepared to convince your prospective financial backer why your business is a good investment, but, more importantly, why you are a good candidate to own and operate it. Many applicants are unaware that the interview is a valuable occasion for learning about the investment firm or lender. Following are some questions you might find valuable:

- What other companies has the investor or lender financed?
- How successful were they?
- What were the payback arrangements?
- What advice or services does the company provide besides supplying money?
- Does the investor want to actively participate in the management of the business?
- If so, how?

Think of the interview, in part, as a fact-finding mission. Even though your main objective is to convince the investor why your business is an attractive investment target, you should also expect the investor to convince you why his firm is an attractive source for securing funds.

The interviewing process frequently involves several personal appearances, sometimes before more than one interviewer.

1. **The screening interview.** A screening interview may be conducted as a preliminary to the final interview. It is sometimes informal, e.g., over lunch, and usually brief (no longer than an hour). The successful candidates who survive the screening interview are invited back for a second interview.

2. **The selection interview.** The selection interview may last several hours, and often results in the eventual rejection or acceptance of the proposal.

3. **The multi-participant interview.** Sometimes, a company deems it advisable to have candidates interviewed by several members of the investment team. In this case, you may expect to be passed along from one interviewer to another, usually in ascending order on the organization chart.

4. **The selection committee.**   On occasion, the firm will have a committee of three or more interview the applicant at the same time. The committee will typically consist of a financial expert, a management expert, and someone familiar with the industry in which the business will be operated.

Preparing for the Interview

Successful interviews result in part from an understanding of the interview process and adequate preparation on the part of the applicant. Following are some guidelines for a successful interview:

1. **Learn about the investment company.**   Find out as much information as you can about the investor or lender. Talk to other companies who have been funded or financed by the firm. See if you can discover how the firm operates, what type of payback they might expect, and the questions they will ask during the interview.

2. **Review the venture proposal.**   Being able to elaborate on the information contained in your proposal résumé warrants some time and effort in preparation for the interview.

3. **Dress appropriately.**   Formal, conservative clothing, such as a tailored suit, is appropriate for both men and women in most situations. It is almost impossible to be overdressed for the interview, but perilous to be underdressed. Formal attire shows you take the job seriously. Women are well advised to wear suits, dresses, or skirts. Never wear jeans, even if they are of the designer type.

4. **Be punctual.**   A punctual, well-dressed applicant always makes a great first impression.

5. **Prepare for stress.**   Most of us are naturally nervous before an important meeting. It helps to get a good night's rest before the interview. Set aside plenty of time to get ready, and avoid stimulants like coffee or soft drinks containing caffeine.

6. **Bring evidence.** Bring any evidence that supports the data and conclusions in your proposal. You may also be asked to show items such as a business license, the franchise agreement, or other official documents relevant to the proposed business.

7. **Be confident.** Act with confidence; confront the interviewer with interest and enthusiasm, and remember to maintain eye contact. Present a firm handshake.

9

Selecting a Source

On a sultry Sunnyvale afternoon in autumn, Jeff B. resigned his secure position as a dealer representative for a well-known computer manufacturer and decided to go into business for himself. He settled on a franchise from a young, up-and-coming outfit which had been franchising for only a few months but had already established a dozen outlets. The initial investment required to open one of these franchises was about $105,000.

Jeff did not own a home or any other source of financial equity. To swing the deal, he would need financial backing. He first spoke with a bank loan officer affiliated with the franchising company. This bank had made an arrangement with the company to provide financial assistance to creditworthy franchisees. After studying the loan, Jeff found that his total payback would amount to about three times the initial funding.

Before making a decision, he ran a small classified ad in the financial section of his local statewide edition of the *Wall*

Street Journal. The ad offered a partnership opportunity in his proposed computer business franchise. It ran only one day, but over the next week, Jeff received 30 phone calls from prospective investors. After the initial conversations, he mailed out eight copies of his venture proposal.

He also wrote to the National Association of Small Business Investment Companies to obtain the names and addresses of SBICs in his state.

A week later, he received a call from one of the investors to whom he had mailed a proposal, requesting a meeting over lunch. The business lunch led to another more formal meeting at the investor's office, scheduled for the following week. In the meantime, a computer printout of SBICs arrived in the mail, and he began contacting a few which seemed promising.

After several lengthy meetings, the prospective investor, an independent venture capitalist, presented a proposal of his own. He would stake Jeff's franchise in return for a 49 percent ownership in the business. Jeff would pay out about half of the profits of the business in the form of quarterly dividends over a period of five years. He would also have to promise to buy back the investor's stock at the end of that period for a guaranteed price. The investment would be made in two "rounds," based on how closely the business's actual performance matched the projection. The proposal was conditioned on the franchisor approving the investor as a partner in the business.

There was one important hitch. If the business failed to make the guaranteed payout by the end of five years, the investor would have the right to buy out Jeff's 51% of the business for the nominal sum of one dollar.

After analyzing the proposed payout and internal rate of return, Jeff found that he would be paying back about two and half times the original amount of the investment.

By this time, he had received a reply from one of the SBICs to whom he had mailed broadcast letters. At an initial meeting, he learned that the investment company could lend him money at a rate lower than the interest charged by the bank.

Either the bank loan or the SBIC funds would be strung out over a lengthy period, making it easier to make the payback. However, the total amount paid out would be high. In contrast, the investor's money would have to be paid back quickly. But once he made the payout, Jeff would have total ownership and no debt service. He would have to sacrifice more in the short term but would reap greater rewards over the long haul.

After careful consideration, Jeff decided to go with the venture capitalist.

As time went by, the business fared slightly better than the projection, and Jeff was able to distribute dividends to his investor. But in the second quarter of the fifth year, the entire computer industry underwent an inexplicable slump. Jeff's franchise stayed afloat, but he was unable to make the final payout.

Without hesitating, the venture capitalist exercised his option to buy Jeff out, and overnight, Jeff's great American dream vanished like lost data in a faulty computer's memory.

The point of this real-life entrepreneurial nightmare is not to prejudice you against independent venture capitalists, but to illustrate some of the important factors that should enter into the selection of a financing source. To be sure, many enterprises funded by venture capitalists have very agreeable outcomes. But you should realize that most businesses in which a venture capital group invests do not fulfill the expectations of either the business owner or the investor. That's because venture capitalists primarily fund high-risk enterprises.

RISK VERSUS RETURN

A typical venture capitalist is seeking a very high return, possibly 200 percent to 300 percent of the initial investment, paid out in a relatively short period. That degree of return is associated only with the riskiest ventures. As a hedge against potential disaster, the venture capitalist may insist on an option to take over the business when and if it takes a disastrous downward plunge.

You might also bear in mind that the venture capitalist in Jeff's example was a small-time, independent investor, not affiliated with any investment company or venture capital group. In this case, the blame for the loss of his business lies on Jeff's shoulders, for not paying enough attention to the investor's style, personality, and *modus operandi*. In short, Jeff was so anxious to close the deal that he overlooked potential drawbacks.

Moreover, the investor was merely protecting his investment. All along, what he wanted was a return on his investment, not to own a computer business. In fact, Jeff's investor was almost as unhappy with the outcome as Jeff. Almost. After all, the investor now owned the business, for better or worse. All Jeff had left were shattered dreams.

In any dealing with an independent investor, envision a caution sign sitting on the conference table between you and your erstwhile financial backer. A small-time investor is literally a personal partner in your business, whether or not he actively participates in its management. When a partnership turns sour, the outcome does not often suit either party.

The case history of Jeff B. points out several other considerations that should enter into the selection decision.

EVALUATING YOUR OPTIONS

In the previous chapter, we examined four sources for financing the franchise: the Small Business Administration, SBICs and MESBICs, venture capital groups, and independent investors. In the next chapter, we will explore a fifth: the franchisor. But our present focus is confined to third-party resources, ones that are not party to the franchise agreement.

Each of these resources has certain advantages and drawbacks which must be evaluated with caution (see the comparison chart shown in Figure 16).

EVALUATING SBA FUNDING

The SBA offers two types of assistance. The first is a direct loan, grant, or subsidy. This type of funding is not always available.

Figure 16

A Comparison of the Advantages
and Drawbacks of Various Funding Sources

Source	Time to Fund	Advantages	Drawbacks
SBA	3–6 mos.	Low interest rate Exclusive focus on small businesses Preference for franchises	Precise timing required Lengthy payout period Some collateral usually required Funds often not available
SBA-Bank Participation Program	1–3 mos.	Low or rea- sonable rate Preference for franchises Funds usually readily available	Lengthy payout period Some collateral may be required
SBIC/ MESBIC	2–4 mos.	Reasonable rate on loans Preference for franchises Investment money available Grants and subsidies available for minorities	Lengthy payout period Moderately slow to process Usually very selective Funds not always available
Venture Capital Groups	3–6 mos.	Short payout period Collateral not required	High payout Ownership must usually be shared Amounts under $100,000 not available Lengthy funding period
Independent Investors	1–3 mos.	Quick funding possible Collateral not required	Ownership must usually be shared Management must often be shared

When the money supply is depleted, there is often a long dry spell between funding periods.

When a regional office of the SBA receives funds from the federal government, they are quickly committed to the first applicants who qualify. Not uncommonly small business owners form long lines outside their local SBA offices on the day after new funds are announced.

Thus, timing is critical. To obtain direct assistance from the SBA, you must act promptly as soon as it is announced that funds are available. But if your timing is right, and your credit is in good standing, your chances of receiving assistance are very good.

The main advantage to SBA funding is that this money is specifically earmarked for small business owners like yourself. The government is not looking for a big payout, or to take over your business.

A second advantage is the low rate, normally lower than any other source of financing. In rare instances, the SBA has made outright grants which do not have to be paid back at all.

A drawback to direct SBA assistance is the critical timing required to get in on the action. If your financial search does not coincide with the one–to–three day period in which SBA funds are available, you might end up growing a white beard waiting for the next round of financing.

The second, and more viable, type of SBA assistance is an indirect loan made through the SBA-bank participation program. Under this program, a conventional lending institution extends a regular business loan which is guaranteed by the SBA. If you should default on the loan, the SBA agrees to compensate the bank for its loss.

Because the money is the bank's, not the government's, this type of loan is usually readily available throughout the year. A second advantage of an SBA-guaranteed loan is that you have the pick of different lending institutions. Various banks, savings and loan associations, and finance companies participate in the program.

A potential drawback is that some type of collateral may be required to qualify. However, the amount is likely to be much less than the collateral required for a conventional loan. Some banks offer SBA-guaranteed loans based on twice the amount of collateral supplied.

If you are not looking for a great deal of money, an SBA-guaranteed loan has an additional advantage. You can usually borrow relatively small amounts, under $100,000. Most venture capitalists will consider only investments of $100,000 or more.

EVALUATING SBICs AND MESBICs

Small Business Investment Companies often have more than one type of funding available. They may make SBA-type loans, based on competitive rates, or they may invest in a business by purchasing a percentage of its ownership. Like a participating bank, the SBIC is licensed by the SBA to lend money to small businesses.

The money comes from the investment company's membership, usually private investors pooling their money to make a profit. However, the group is usually interested in a diversity of investments, including stocks, treasury bills, commodities, and money market funds.

As a result, an SBIC typically confines its lending activity to a few select businesses. To receive funding, your proposal will have to compete favorably with other business plans vying for the SBIC's limited loan dollars. But if you have a particularly successful franchisor in a dynamic growth industry, the SBIC might be interested in a direct investment in your franchise.

A MESBIC (the minority enterprise version of an SBIC) also makes low-interest loans and direct investments, but additionally, may grant an outright subsidy to a minority-owned business.

A big advantage to SBIC and MESBIC funding is that these sources expressly favor franchises. This attitude is based on the high survival rate of franchise outlets, as well as the training and assistance provided by franchisors. A minority business owner with a franchise is in an excellent position to receive financial aid from a licensed MESBIC.

EVALUATING VENTURE CAPITALISTS _____

Of all the various sources of small business funding, by far the most glamorous is the venture capital community. Few businessmen have not heard the story of how entrepreneurs in the microelectronics industry earned enormous fortunes overnight, on the shoulders of risk-taking venture capitalists.

Many small business people think of venture capitalists first, when they consider sources of cash infusion. But, as Jeff B. learned the hard way, investment money from a venture capitalist may have pitfalls as well as advantages.

Like the ventures they fund, venture capitalists occur in many forms. A typical venture capital firm is a group of wealthy investors who put money into a common fund managed by a handful of advisors. The investors are more interested in the amount of their return than in the specific businesses in which the managers invest.

A variation of this kind of investment group is the information pool. Rather than making final investment decisions, the managers of the fund simply make recommendations to the group's membership. Individual members may choose a specific investment target from a published list.

Other sources of venture capital include insurance companies, management consulting groups, and major corporations with large cash surpluses.

All venture capitalists have at least one common objective: an extraordinarily high return. What sets a venture capitalist apart from other investors is his focus on high-risk, high-yield business investments, rather than "safe" investments like stocks or treasury bills. Venture capitalists want to get in quickly, realize a big return, and get out. They are almost never involved in a business for the long haul.

For all these reasons, the payout plan includes large payments made over a fairly short period. It also usually includes partial ownership in the business and a guaranteed buyback at a predetermined price.

If your franchisor is a young company, short on history but long on future, a venture capitalist offers the advantage of funding that might otherwise be difficult to acquire. Moreover, you do not normally need any collateral to obtain the funds. In return for the large payout, the venture capitalist is sharing your risk.

Another advantage is that the venture capitalist usually wants out fairly quickly. Once you have made the final payout, the business and its profits are 100 percent yours. With a long-term business loan, your obligation lingers on for decades.

A potential drawback is the arduous application process. Your proposal, your personal credentials, your designated management team, your franchisor, and the industry itself will undergo rigorous scrutiny before a venture capitalist will make a funding decision. The process will take a minimum of three to six months to complete.

If your franchise agreement requires you to open your doors for business in sixty days, you probably will not have time to negotiate a venture capital deal. However, your franchisor may be willing to grant you an extension, if he believes firmly enough in your serious intent and your personal qualifications. Alternatively, you might arrange to defer amounts that are payable to your franchisor, such as the initial fee, inventory purchases, etc.

Perhaps the biggest pitfall to venture capital money is organizational complexity. The capital group may insist on having a designated member of its own team participating in the management of your business. To be sure, they will be represented on your board of directors. You might also be required to give the group an option to take over the business if you are unable to make your payout obligations.

THE DECISION

As you weigh the risks, benefits, advantages, and drawbacks of each funding source, the best answer for your particular situation will make itself obvious. Ask yourself the following questions before you make the final decision:

1. **How much funding do I really need?** If the amount of funding you require is less than $100,000, most venture

capital groups will not be interested. The potential payout is simply not worth their bother, even at a high rate of return. Even SBA-guaranteed loans have established minimums. In most cases, a loan under $40,000 will be considered too trivial.

2. **How long do I want to make the payback?** A loan from the SBA, a participating bank, or an SBIC can typically be structured to allow from 15 to 30 years to pay back the original funds plus a reasonably low interest. With a venture capital investment, you will normally have from three to five years to pay the initial investment plus you reap the benefits of a high return. Another way of looking at it is that you're free of the venture capitalist after a few short years of modest sacrifice, whereas you and the bank may be partners for almost the rest of your life.

3. **Which source best complements your own personality and business style?** Ultimately, your favored funding source should be the one you can work with best. Even banks and government agencies have personality quirks and business styles in the persona of its officers. In more ways than one, your financial backer will be your partner in progress. You should seek that delicate chemistry wherein your own personality traits, management behavior, and business objectives blend smoothly and effortlessly with your partner's.

SECTION
3

Franchisors
Who
Finance

10

The
Financing
Franchisor

When Peter and Jennifer L. went into business for themselves, they did not seriously consider any other type of entity but a franchise. To them, a franchise meant a "safe" small business, much like a treasury bill represents a safe security to an investor. They recognized that, no matter what market they entered, they would need training, guidance, and the type of knowledge only someone experienced in the business could give them. They wanted to get into business quickly and painlessly, avoiding the trial-and-error pitfalls that doom most small business start-ups at the outset.

Embarking on their search for the ideal franchisor, they narrowed the field to companies with three characteristics:

1. Franchisors that had been in business at least five years
2. Franchisors that had established at least a dozen outlets, not including company-owned stores
3. Franchisors that offered some form of financial assistance

Happily, they found thousands of franchise opportunities and hundreds of franchisors meeting the minimum qualifications. Some, they found, will finance only the initial franchise fee. Others were willing to finance the fee plus a portion of the investment for commercial space, opening inventory, and working capital. Still others said they would finance the entire start-up investment if Peter and Jennifer could convince them of their motivation, personal integrity, and ambition.

Finally, the couple settled on a convenience store franchise with a well entrenched franchisor that had established several hundred stores in a history spanning more than two decades. The franchisor financed the entire investment, including the site, fixtures, and opening inventory.

A few days after signing the franchise agreement, Peter and Jennifer had their next door neighbors over for dinner to celebrate. The wife, Heather, commented: "You know, it sounds to me like you and Peter bought yourself jobs."

Jennifer smiled, but did not reply.

Twelve years later, Heather had finally advanced to an assistant foreman at the semiconductor factory where she worked. Her husband was still estimating auto repair work, after a six month layoff.

Peter and Jennifer had just made the last payment on their franchise loan. If things continue to go well over the next three or four years, they plan to open two more stores.

Why would a franchisor put up the money to put you in business for yourself? For one thing, you may be in business for yourself, but certainly not by yourself.

A franchisor with numerous outlets has a demonstrable

success formula. The company believes in its formula and knows how well it works. When it sells a new franchise, it is more interested in finding the right personalities, than another initial franchise fee.

For another thing, successful franchisors have franchise revenues to re-invest. In their particular businesses, no investment is better than more franchise outlets.

For three reasons a franchisor might offer financing: (1) to encourage rapid expansion, (2) to derive additional profits, and (3) to re-invest surplus cash.

A CATALYST OF GROWTH

Far more people want to own franchises than have the money to buy them. A franchisor may offer financial assistance to help establish new outlets, hoping to generate strength in numbers. Many of the competitive advantages to franchising are co-operative in nature.

For example, contributions by numerous franchisees to a co-op ad fund permits the company to conduct major ad campaigns on a par with industry giants. Franchisees also enjoy the benefit of co-op purchasing power, taking advantage of volume discounts on inventory and supplies.

To build a powerful co-op system quickly, a franchisor may finance new outlets to make it easier for prospective franchisees to get into the business.

AN ANCILLARY PROFIT CENTER

Another reason why a franchisor may offer financing is to diversify its sources of revenue. By lending money to franchisees, or offering credit terms for purchases of equipment, inventory, or real estate, the franchisor realizes additional profits from the interest charged. On the financing of equipment or machinery purchases, the company also gains depreciation benefits.

A franchisor who commands a low royalty is most likely to have an internal financing program.

A REINVESTMENT STRATEGY

Any company that enjoys extraordinary success has a unique, if enviable, problem: a surplus of cash. The reason cash reserves are a problem is that they are essentially unproductive. Cash in a bank account produces a poor payout, sometimes lower than the current inflation rate. Most companies would rather put idle cash to work by reinvesting it in high-return opportunities. Therefore, the franchisor derives supplemental profits from both interest charges and new franchise royalties.

THE CRITERIA

When dealing with an established franchisor who offers financing, be aware that the most important factor from the franchisor's point of view is your personal integrity. Each franchise has a so-called "ideal franchisee profile:" a description of the personality traits and work background that the franchisor has found contribute to success in that particular line of business. Ambition, drive, motivation, perseverance, and honesty are on every list.

Some, but not all, franchise finance programs are like conventional business loans. They have a set term, e.g., 15 years, and a fixed or variable interest rate. But unlike a conventional loan, some plans do not actually require good credit standing or collateral.

A third party may be involved, such as a capital investment group or leasing company. The third party puts up the money to finance the business, and the franchisor co-signs to guarantee the loan. The investor realizes depreciation and capitalization benefits. The franchisee gets his own business for no money down. And the franchisor establishes another outlet from which to derive royalty income.

In many respects, a franchising company that finances is leveraging. It is leveraging your entrepreneurial spirit and personal ambition. But in other respects, you are leveraging the franchisor. You are leveraging its past success, its business format, and its cash surplus.

11

The Franchisors Who Finance

This final chapter is devoted to a listing of franchisors who finance. Each one indicated that some form of financing is available, either through the franchisor itself or through a participating third party. Inclusion on this list is based solely on information supplied by the franchisors. Neither the author nor the publisher have any responsibility for the accuracy of that information.

If your primary interest in franchising for free is with franchisors who finance, this list is a good starting point. Good luck, and happy franchising.

──────────────── **AUTO MAINTENANCE** ────────────

AAMCO Transmissions
One Presidential Blvd.
Bala Cynwyd, PA 19004

ABT Service Centers
(801) 972-2065
2339 South 2700 West
Salt Lake City, UT 84119

American International Rent A Car
4801 Spring Valley Road
Dallas, TX 75244

Bingo Scene Magazine
8500 Station Street, Suite 240
Mentor, OH 44060

Budget Rent A Car
(312) 580-5000
200 North Michigan Ave.
Chicago, IL 60656

Building Inspector of America, The
684 Main Street
Wakefield, MA 01880

Custom Auto Touch Up
7435 South Tamiami Tr.
Sarasota, FL 33581

Downey Automobile, Inc.
(615) 899-1610
4105 South Creek Road
Chattanooga, TN 37406

Econo Lube N'Tune
(714) 851-2259
4911 Birch Street, Suite 100
Newport Beach, CA 92660

Goodyear Tire Centers
(216) 796-2121
1144 East Market Street
Akron, OH 44316

Grease'n Go
305 East Main Street, Suite 400
Mesa, AZ 85202

House Master of America
421 Western Union Avenue
Bound Brook, NJ 08805

Jiffy Lube
(301) 298-8200
7008 Security Blvd, Suite 300
Baltimore, MD 21207

King Bear Auto Service Center
(516) 483-3500
1390 Jerusalem Avenue
North Merrick, NY 11566

Lee Myles Transmissions
(800) 631-1699
25 East Spring Valley Avenue
Maywood, NJ 07034

Meineke Discount Mufflers
128 South Tryon, Suite 900
Charlotte, NC 28202

National Autofinders, Inc.
(316) 721-3000
520 South Holland
Wichita, KS 67209

Property Inspection Service
1741 Saratoga Avenue, Suite 106
San Jose, CA 95129

RPM Rent-A-Car System
6000 Sepulveda Blvd.
Van Nuys, CA 91411

Rent A Wreck
(213) 208-7712
10889 Wilshire Blvd., Suite 1260
Los Angeles, CA 90024

Star Technology Windshield Repair
4593 North Broadway
Boulder, CO 80302

Sunshine Polishing Systems Mobile Franchise
(619) 233-3343
4560 Alvarado Canyon Road, Suite 24
San Diego, CA 92120

Triex
66 Palmer Ave.
Bronxville, NY 10708

Tuff-Kote Dinol
P.O. Box 03998
Highland Park, MI 48203-0998

U-Save Auto Rental of America
P.O. Box 1651
Salisbury, NC 28144

Unico Autobody and Paint
(818) 996-2018
7400 Reseda Blvd.
Reseda, CA 91335

Western Auto
(816) 346-4000
2107 Grand Avenue
Kansas City, MO 64108

_____ VACATIONS AND ENTERTAINMENT _____

Adventurent
629 North East 3rd Street
Diania, FL 33004

American Fast Photo & Camera
32100 Telegraph Road
Birmingham, MI 48010

American Safari National R.V. Rental Systems
(305) 666-5866
12550 Biscayne Blvd.
Miami, FL 33181

Atlanta Concessions Systems, Inc.
(305) 925-7223
P.O. Box 2326
Hollywood, FL 33022

Camera America
1404 Gornto Road
Valdosta, GA 31602

Cruise Holidays
(619) 587-0081
3435 Camino Del Rio South, Suite 313
San Diego, CA 92108

Disc Jockey Entertainment
(602) 991-8500
2529 East Indian School Road
Phoenix, AZ 85016

Holiday Inns
(901) 362-4148
3796 Lamar Avenue
Memphis, TN 38195

Instant Photo Corp. of America
20280 Governors Hwy.
Olympia Fields, IL 60461

Neighborhood Video & 1-Hour Photo Center
(818) 885-7887
8739 Shirley Avenue
Northridge, CA 91324

Nelson's Photography Studios, Inc.
(216) 861-4572
41 Colonial Arcade
Cleveland, OH 44115

Sound Tracks Recording Studios
424 Parkway
Sevierville, TN 37862

Travel Travel
(619) 942-1818
679 Encinitas Blvd.
Encinitas, CA 92024

Video Guard
(509) 624-4201
South 312 Post, Suite D
Spokane, WA 99204

Videotrax
(404) 993-7436
10925 Crabapple Road, Suite 201
Roswell, GA 30075

Yogi Bear's Jellystone Park
Leisure Systems, Inc.
Bushkill, PA 18324

---------------------- **BUSINESS** ----------------------

AAA Employment
(813) 577-7011
5533 Central Avenue
St. Petersburg, FL 33710

Abraham & London
(818) 905-1011
P.O. Box 4945
Chatsworth, CA 91313

Accu Copy
200 Mouse Mill Road
Westport, MA 02790

Advantage Payroll Services
800 Center Street
Auburn, ME 04210

Air Brook Limousine
115 West Passaic Street
Rochelle Park, NJ 07662

Ameribiz Employment
(603) 622-3070
167 South River Road
Bedford, NH 03102

American Check Reporting Co., Inc.
(615) 361-1314
1824 Murfresboro Road
Nashville, TN 37217

American College Planning Service
5475 Crestview
Memphis, TN 38134

American Lenders Service Co.
312 East Second Street
Odessa, TX 79760

American Speedy Printing Centers
(800) 521-4002
32100 Telegraph Road
Birmingham, MI 48010

Atlantic Personnel Services
4806 Shelly Drive
Wilmington, NC 28405

Barter Exchange
1106 Clayton Lane, Suite 480 West
Austin, TX 78723

Bailey Employment Service
(203) 261-2908
51 Shelton Road
Monroe, CT 06468

Business Card Express
401 South Woodward Avenue, Suite 350
Birmingham, MI 48011

Business Exchange International, Inc.
(213) 887-2161
4716 Vineland Avenue
North Hollywood, CA 91602

Business & Professional Consultants
(213) 380-8200
3807 Wilshire Blvd., Suite 1732
Los Angeles, CA 90010

Classified Photo Ads
9101 East Kenyon Avenue
Denver, CO 80237

Commercial Services Company
(305) 647-1113
2699 Lee Road, Suite 150
Winter Park, FL 32789

Communications World
14828 West 6th Avenue, Suite 13B
Golden, CO 80401

Comprehensive Accounting
(312) 898-1234
2111 Comprehensive Drive
Aurora, IL 60507

Computer Servicenters, Inc.
(601) 969-9193
P.O. Box 1543
Jackson, MS 39205

Corporate Investment Business Brokers
(602) 266-0100
1515 East Missouri Avenue
Phoenix, AZ 02134

Correct Credit Co.
P.O. Box 537
Howell, NJ 07731

Dental Power
5530 Wisconsin Avenue, Suite 741
Chevy Chase, MD 20815

Division 10
(212) 869-0300
1500 Broadway
New York, NY 10036

Dunhill Personnel System
(516) 741-5081
One Old Country Road
Carle Place, NY 11514

Energy Doctor
(806) 793-3105
4216 50th
Lubbock, TX 79413

Engineering Corporation of America
(206) 622-7696
600 First Avenue, Suite 402
Seattle, WA 98104

F-O-R-T-U-N-E Personnel Consultants
(212) 697-4314
655 Third Avenue, Suite 1805
New York, NY 10017

Gingiss Formalwear
180 North La Salle Street
Chicago, IL 60601

Gold 'N Links
(801) 575-6000
5 Triad Ctr., Suite 625
Salt Lake City, UT 84180

Health Force
(516) 794-4850
1975 Hempstead Tpke.
East Meadow, NY 11554

Insty-Prints
(800) 228-6714
1215 Marshall Street
Minneapolis, MN 55413

International Mergers and Acquisitions
(602) 990-3899
8100 E. Indian School Road, Suite 7
Scottsdale, AZ 85251

K & W Computerized Tax Services
1607 Minnesota Avenue
Kansas City, KS 66102

Kwik-Kopy Printing
(800) 231-4542
One Kwik-Kopy Lane
Cypress, TX 77429

Labor World
5499 North Federal Hwy., Suite D
Boca Raton, FL 33431

Management Center, The
4122 Forest Hill Avenue
Richmond, VA 23225

Marcoin Business Services
(404) 325-1200
1924 Cliff Valley Way
Atlanta, GA 30329

Mifax-Yourtown
(319) 234-4896
3022 Airport Blvd.
Waterloo, IA 50704

Minuteman Press
1640 New Hwy.
Farmingdale, NY 11735

Money Mailer
(714) 898-9111
15472 Chemical Lane
Huntington Beach, CA 92649

National Commerce Exchange, Inc.
(800) 336-4771
6501 Loisdale Court 909
Springfield, VA 22150

National Tenant Network
P.O. Box 1664
Lake Grove, OR 97034

Office Alternative
(800) 262-4181
One Sea Gate, Suite 1001
Toledo, OH 43604

Parson-Bishop National Collections
7870 Camargo Road
Cincinnati, OH 45243

Petro Brokerage & Services
1645 Falmouth Road
Centerville, MA 02632

Phone Master Communications
6691 Owens Drive
Pleasanton, CA 94566

Printing Supermart
(201) 239-0233
532 Bloomfield Avenue
Verona, NJ 07044

Pro Creations Maternity Leasewear
(503) 659-4020
180 North La Salle Street
Chicago, IL 60601

Pro Forma
4705 Van Epps Road
Cleveland, OH 44131

Quik Print
3445 North Webb Road
Wichita, KS 67226

Respond First Aid Systems
(303) 371-6800
P.O. Box 39398
Denver, CO 80239

Résumé Works, The
1500 Katella, Suite 6
Orange, CA 92667

Romac
(800) 341-0263
183 Middle Street, 3rd Floor
Portland, ME 04112

Room-Mate Referral Service Center
(405) 631-5706
8909 South Western Avenue
Oklahoma City, OK 73139

Roth Young Personnel Service
1500 Broadway
New York, NY 10036

Sanford Rose Associates
(800) 321-2174
265 South Main Street
Akron, OH 44308

Service Coffee
17895-G Sky Park Circle Drive
Irvine, CA 92714

Service Personnel/Temp Co.
P.O. Box 87
Auburntown, TN 37016

Sexton Educational Centers
443 East Third Avenue
Roselle, NJ 07203

Sign Express
P.O. Box 309
Bethel, CT 06801

Stuffit Direct Mail
12450 Automobile Blvd.
Clearwater, FL 33520

Sylvan Learning Centers
2400 Presidents Drive
Montgomery, AL 36103-5605

Temp Force
1975 Hempstead Tpke.
East Meadows, NY 11544

Temporaries
1308 19th Street Northwest
Washington, DC 20036

Timesavers Temporary Personnel
(408) 734-9940
1296 Lawrence Station Road
Sunnyvale, CA 94086

TLC Nursing Center
4480 North Shallowford Road, Suite 207
Atlanta, GA 30338

Trans America Printing
1286 Citizens Pky.
Morrow, GA 30260

Triple Check Income Tax Service
(213) 849-2273
727 South Main Street
Burbank, CA 91506

Western Vinyl Repair
3000 South Jamaica Court, Suite 225
Aurora, CO 80014

MAINTENANCE, HOUSEHOLD FURNISHING, AND ACCESSORIES

Aerowest/Westair Washroom Sanitation Service
25100 South Normandie
Harbor City, CA 90710

Almost Heaven Hot Tubs
(304) 497-3163
Route 5 FF
Renick, WV 24966

Aquapura
26 Arcadia Road
Old Greenwich, CT 96807

American Leak Detection
(619) 320-8273
1750 East Arenas Road, Suite 1
Palm Springs, CA 92262

Americlean
6602 South Frontage Road
Billings, MT 59101

Americlean Mobile Power Wash & Restoration
(800) 262-9274
50 Sandoe Road
Gettysburg, PA 17325

Bucket Brigade
2043 Creekside Drive
Wheaton, IL 60187

Buning The Florist
(305) 463-7660
801 Southwest 20th Way
Ft. Lauderdale, FL 33312

Clean Co
2211 West County Road, C-2
St. Paul, MN 55113

Coit Drapery and Carpet Cleaners
(415) 342-6023
897 Hinckley Road
Burlingame, CA 94010

Coverall
(619) 584-1911
4110 North Scottsdale Road, Suite 115
Scottsdale, AZ 85251

Deck The Walls
(713) 890-5900
P.O. Box 4586
Houston, TX 77210-4586

Duraclean International, Inc.
(312) 945-2000
2151 Waukegan Road
Deerfield, IL 60015

Framin' Place—Frame Factory
(713) 467-9513
9605 Dalecrest
Houston, TX 77080

Guarantee Carpet Cleaning & Dye Co.
(904) 733-8211
2953 Powers Avenue
Jacksonville, FL 32207

Homeworks
1800 Robert Fulton Drive
Reston, VA 22091

Jani-King
(800) 552-5264
4950 Keller Springs, Suite 190
Dallas, TX 75248

JaniMaster
44 Pine Knoll Drive, Suite B
Greenville, SC 29615

Jiffiwash
(415) 543-3483
P.O. Box 2489
San Francisco, CA 94126

Maid Brigade
850 Indian Tr., Box 1901
Atlanta, GA 30247

Maids, The America's Maid Service
5015 Underwood Avenue
Omaha, NE 68132

Maintenance King, Inc.
(800) 526-1447
89 West 43rd Street
Bayonne, NJ 97002

Molly Maid
(800) 331-4600
3001 South State Street
Ann Arbor, MI 48104

National Maintenance Contractors
(106) 881-0500
4024 148th Northeast
Redmond, WA 98052

O'Malley's Flowers
(818) 784-1897
15303 Ventura Blvd., Suite 700
Sherman Oaks, CA 91403

Professional Carpet Systems
5250 Old Dixie Hwy.
Forest Park, GA 30050

Roof-Vac
(201) 232-1750
2143 Morris Avenue
Union, NJ 07083

Sara Care Services
(800) 351-2273
1200 Golden Key Circle, Suite 368
El Paso, TX 79925

Service-Maids Industries, Inc.
(303) 988-9000
2255 South Wadsworth, Suite 202
Lakewood, CO 80227

Service Master
(800) 852-1212
2300 Warrenville Road
Downers Grove, IL 60515

Servpro
(800) 826-9586
P.O. Box 5001
Rancho Cordova, CA 95670

Siesta Sleep Shop
386 Lindelof Ave.
Stoughton, MA 02072

Soap Opera, The
1535 Grimmet Drive
Shreveport, LA 71107

Sparkle Wash
26851 Richmond Road
Cleveland, OH 44146

Stanley Steemer Carpet Cleaner
(614) 764-2007
5500 Stanley Steemer Parkway
Dublin, OH 43017

Steamatic
1601 109th Street
Grand Prairie, TX 75050

Sunrise Maintenance Systems
(602) 778-4224
122 North Cortez, Suite 317
Prescott, AZ 86301

Surface Specialists
Route 3, Box 72
Isanti, MN 55040

Ultra Brite Blind Cleaning
(313) 476-1627
32433 West 8 Mile Road
Livonia, MI 48150

Ultra Wash
(713) 796-0071
8100 Cambridge Street, Suite 121
Houston, TX 77054

Wash-Bowl Home Style Coin Laundries Stores
(305) 264-6060
4101 Southwest 73rd Avenue
Miami, FL 33155

Wicks 'N' Sticks
(713) 890-5900
P.O. Box 4586
Houston, TX 77210

Window Man, The
711 Rigsbee Avenue
Durham, NC 27701

World Bazaar
1860-74 Peachtree Road, Northwest
Atlanta, GA 30357

REMODELLING, CONSTRUCTION AND REAL ESTATE

Archadeck
P.O. Box 5185
Richmond, VA 23220

B-Dry System
(216) 867-2576
1341 Copley Road
Akron, OH 44320

Century 21 Real Estate
(714) 752-7521
P.O. Box 19565
Irvine, CA 92714

Energy Doctor
(806) 793-3105
4216 50th
Lubbock, TX 79413

Facelifters
83 North Lively Blvd.
Elk Grove Village, IL 60007

Help-U-Sell, Inc.
(801) 355-1177
110 West 300 South, Suite 238
Salt Lake City, UT 84101

Hometrend
3600 South Beeler Street, Suite 300
Denver, CO 80237

Just Closets
(415) 457-3961
25 Pelican Way
San Rafael, CA 94901

Natural Log Homes, Inc.
(904) 396-1662
3515 St. Augustine Road
Jacksonville, FL 32207

Plywood Ranch Industries, Inc.
(617) 848-7260
280 Quincy Avenue
Braintree, MA 02184

ProTech Restoration, Inc.
(805) 966-7479
26 East Cota Street
Santa Barbara, CA 93101

Rapid Economical Construction Systems Corp.
3510 Biscayne Blvd., Suite 203
Miami, FL 33137

Re/Max
(303) 770-5531
P.O. Box 3907
5251 South Quebec
Englewood, CO 80155

Re-Modelers Unlimited
245 West Street, Route 67
Seymour, CT 06483

Real Estate One
745 South Garfield Avenue
Traverse City, MI 49684

Realty World
12500 Fair Lakes Circle
Fairfax, VA 22033

Red Carpet Real Estate Services, Inc.
(619) 571-7181
P.O. Box 85660
San Diego, CA 92138

State Wide Real Estate
P.O. Box 297
Escanaba, MI 49829

Tempaco, Inc.
(305) 898-3456
1701 Alden Road
Orlando, FL 32854

Tile Roofers, Inc.
(417) 736-2080
P.O. Box 214
Strafford, MO 65757

―――――――――――― **HEALTH AND BEAUTY** ――――――――――――

Aloette
345 Lancaster Avenue
Malvern, PA 19355

Command Performance
(617) 470-2570
355 Middlesex Avenue
Wilmington, MA 01887

Dwight Dental Care
(914) 233-6028
280 Railroad Avenue
Greenwich, CT 06830

Fantastic Body Wrap Salons
(303) 423-3438
8433 Chase Drive
Arvada, CO 80003

Fortunate Life Weight Loss Centers
P.O. Box 5604
Charlottesville, VA 22905

Gloria Stevens Figure Salons
(617) 848-7380
10 Forbes Road
Braintree, MA 02184

Great Earth Vitamin Store
(213) 516-9570
19603 South Vermont Avenue
Torrance, CA 90502

Great Expectations Precision Haircutters
125 South Service Road
Jericho, NY 11753

Hair Crafters
125 South Service Road
Jericho, NY 11753

i Natural Cosmetics
(215) 576-6348
355 Middlesex Avenue
Wilmington, MA 02193

Jacquie's Place
1280 South Pompano Pky, Suite 20
Pompano Beach, FL 33069

Joan M. Cable's La Femmina Beauty Salon
3301 Hempstead Tpke.
Long Island, NY 11756

Lemon Tree, The
(516) 794-6745
3301 Hempstead Tpke.
Long Island, NY 11756

MacLevy Products Corp.
(800) 221-0277
43-23 91st Place
Elmhurst, NY 11373

NuVision Optical
P.O. Box 2600
Flint, MI 48501

Omnidentix Business Systems Corp.
(617) 329-7474
555 High Street
Westwood, MA 02090

Pearle Vision Center
2534 Royal Lane
Dallas, TX 75229

Sun Tan-Tanarama
(901) 682-7712
474 Perkins Exit, Suite 204
Memphis, TN 38117

Texas State Optical
(214) 241-3381
2534 Royal Lane
Dallas, TX 75229

Waist Basket, The
(504) 469-3848
2002 20th Street, Suite A101
Kenner, LA 70062

Woman's World Health Spas
(617) 926-6200
210–216 Dexter Avenue
Watertown, MA 02172

──────────────── FOODS ────────────────

All-V's Sandwiches
(303) 781-1663
P.O. Box 4068
Highlands Ranch, CO 80216

Ben Franks
1300 Hancock Street
Redwood City, CA 94063

Big Orange
(608) 269-2233
431 Holtan Street
Sparta, WI 54656

Big Pete's, Inc.
(304) 925-9713
3516 McCorkle Ave.
Charleston, WV 20304

Blimpie
(212) 888-1800
1414 Avenue of the Americas, 15th Floor
New York, NY 10019

Carter's Nuts
(212) 732-6887
215 West 34th Street
New York, NY 10001

Carvel
(914) 969-7200
201 Saw Mill River Road
Yonkers, NY 10701

Cozzoli's Pizza
(305) 358-5086
555 North East 15th, Suite 33-D
Miami, FL 33132

Delaware Punch Syrup Co.
(512) 349-4571
506 West Rhapsody
San Antonio, TX 78216

Donut Inn
(213) 888-2220
6355 Topanga Canyon Blvd., Suite 403
Woodland Hills, CA 91367

Drakes's Salad Bar Restaurant
(602) 994-0630
7575 East Main Street, Suite 204
Scottsdale, AZ 85251

Dunkin' Donuts
(617) 961-4000
P.O. Box 317
Randolph, MA 02368

Food-N-Fuel
(612) 786-5151
8500 Lexington Avenue
North Billercia, MA 01862

Foster's Donuts
c/o Horn Realty
3585 Maple Street, Suite 120
Ventura, CA 93003

Grandma Buffalo's Chips
(408) 449-5000
24 Pine Hill Way
Monterey, CA 93940

Honor Shoppe
(715) 832-1525
1708 West Gate Road
Eau Claire, WI 54701

Ice Castle
169 South State
Orem, UT 84058

Ice Cream Churn
P.O. Box 759
Byron, GA 31008-0759

I Love Yogurt Shoppes
(214) 788-1580
12770 Coit Road, Suite 415A
Dallas, TX 75251

International Aromas
(603) 623-6198
1000 East Industrial Drive
Manchester, NH 03102

International House of Pancakes
(213) 982-2620
6837 Lankershim Blvd., North
Hollywood, CA 91605

Jiffy Shoppes
8545 Ashwood Drive
Capitol Heights, MD 20027

Jo-Ann's Nut House/Chez Chocolate
657 Line Road
Aberdeen, NJ 07747

Joyce's Submarine Sandwiches
(303) 344-1674
1527 Havana
Aurora, CO 80010

L.L. Peach Convenience Food Store
101 Billercia Avenue North
Billercia, MA 01862

Mamacita's
(213) 424-1323
388 East Willow Street
Long Beach, CA 90806

Meyer's Sandwich Shoppes, Inc.
(216) 883-0700
3055 East 63rd Street
Cleveland, OH 44127

Paradise Donuts
(816) 826-8981
211 Thompson Blvd.
Sedalia, MO 65301

Pepperidge Farm
542 Westport Avenue
Norwalk, CT 96856

Phanny's Phudge Emporium
571 North Poplar Avenue, Suite B
Orange, CA 92668

Pizza Man "He Delivers"
(213) 933-8586
6930 Tujunga Avenue, North
Hollywood, CA 91605

Ponderosa Steakhouse
(513) 890-6400
P.O. Box 578
Dayton, OH 45401

Primos Deli Cafe & Jan Drakes Garden Cafe
21622 North 14th Avenue
Phoenix, AZ 85027

Priscilla Adams Food Shoppes
(617) 426-0108
185 Devonshire Street
Boston, MA 02110

Rosati's Pizza
(312) 893-4090
1000 Morse Avenue
Schaumburg, IL 60193

Sabrett Western Distributors, Inc.
190 El Camino Real
Milbrea, CA 94030

Sam The Chicken Man
118 South Clinton, Suite 300
Iowa City, IA 52241

7-Eleven
P.O. Box 719
2828 North Haskell Avenue
Dallas, TX 75204-0719

Shrimp Boat, The
P.O. Box 4437
Biloxi, MS 39531

Simms Sandwich Shops Dev. Corp.
(303) 233-4344
727 Simms Street
Golden, CO 80401

Snappy Tomato Pizza
1950 Radcliff Drive
Cincinnati, OH 45204

Sonic Drive-Ins
6800 North Bryant
Oklahoma City, OK 73121

Southern Maid Donut Shop
(214) 272-6425
3615 Cavalier Drive
Garland, TX 75042

Super Sub Shops
(901) 682-7712
474 Perkins Exit, Suite 204
Memphis, TN 38117

Taco Bonita
(616) 473-2129
Route 2, Grange Road
Berrien Springs, MI 49103

Taco John's
(307) 635-0101
714 West 20th Street
Cheyenne, WY 82001

Tour Ice
1330 Ford Street
Colorado Springs, CO 80915

Tra-Hans Candies, Inc.
603 Beverly Drive
Brandon, FL 33511

Uncle Tony's Pizza & Pasta
17-L Airport Plaza
1800 Post Road
Warwick, RI 02886

Vista Restaurants
(913) 537-0100
1191 Tuttle Creek Blvd.
Manhattan, KS 66502

White Hen Pantry
(312) 833-3100
660 Industrial Drive
Elmhurst, IL 60126

Suggested Reading

Foster, Dennis L., *The Rating Guide to Franchises*, Facts on File, New York, 1988.

Foster, Dennis L., *The Complete Franchise Book*, Prima Publishing, Sacramento (CA), 1987.

Glickman, Gladys, *Franchising*, Matthew Bender, New York, 1976.

Lewis, Mack, *How to Franchise Your Business*, Pilot Books, New York, 1974.

Modica, Alfred, *Franchising*, Quick Fox, New York, 1981.

Seltz, David D., *How to Get Started in Your Own Franchised Business*, Farnsworth, New York, 1967.

Vaughn, Charles, *Franchising*, D. C. Heath, Lexington (MA), 1974.

Vesper, K. H., *New Venture Strategies,* Prentice-Hall, Englewood Cliffs (NJ), 1980.

White, R. M., *The Entrepreneur's Manual,* Chilton, Radnor (PA), 1977.

————, *The 1987 Franchise Annual Handbook and Directory,* Info Press, Lewiston (NY), 1987.

————, *Advice for Persons Who Are Considering an Investment in a Franchise Business,* U.S. Government Printing Office, Washington, DC, 1987.

————, *Are You Ready For Franchising?,* U.S. Government Printing Office, Washington, DC, 1974.

————, *Directory of Franchise Organizations,* New York, Pilot Books, 1987.

————, *Focal Points on Franchising,* U.S. Government Printing Office, Washington, DC, 1987.

————, *Franchising in the Economy,* U.S. Government Printing Office, Washington, DC, 1987.

————, *Franchise Opportunities Handbook,* U.S. Government Printing Office, Washington, DC, 1987.

————, *SBA Business Loans,* U.S. Government Printing Office, Washington, DC, 1987.

Appendix

Financial Plan Worksheets

The following worksheets provide a blueprint for organizing the essential information of a successful franchise financial plan. Use them to gather, prepare, and document the data from which your own plan will materialize. The last worksheet to prepare is the Abstract, which summarizes the remaining sections of the plan. In the final document, the Abstract should appear first.

TITLE PAGE

A BUSINESS PROPOSAL FOR

_____

Prepared by:

Owner's name: _____

Business name: _____

Address: _____

_____

Telephone: _____

ABSTRACT

1. What is the name of the proposed business? _____

_____

2. Franchisee's name: _____

3. Franchisor's name: _____

4. Briefly describe the type of business in which the franchise operation will be engaged: _____

_____

_____

5. What is the total amount of financial assistance that you will require? $_____

6. How will the money be spent?

   a. _____

   b. _____

   c. _____

   d. _____

   e. _____

7. Where will the proposed franchise outlet(s) be located?

_____

8. Briefly describe the market for the proposed business:

_____

_____

_____

9. Summarize the demographics of the typical customer of the proposed outlet. Include only the items that are relevant to the business.

        Gender: _____

        Age: _____

        Income: _____

        Profession: _____

        Education: _____

10. Estimate the total number of customers in your proposed marketing area:_____ customers.

11. Estimate the total size of the market in annual sales:
    $_____

12. Summarize the projected pretax profits for each of the first three years of the business.

    a. First year pretax profit: $_____

    b. Second year pretax profit: $_____

    c. Third year pretax profit: $_____

BUSINESS STATEMENT

Business Objectives

1. State the amount of financial assistance you are seeking:
   $_____

2. State the purpose of the financial assistance:
   a. _____
   b. _____
   c. _____

3. State the marketing objective of the business: a _____ %
   share of the _____ market, within two years.

4. State the profit objectives of the business:
   a. It is anticipated that the business will reach the break-even
      point after _____ six months.
   b. The business will realize a pretax (profit/loss) of $_____
      at the end of the first fiscal year.
   c. The business will realize a pretax (profit/loss) of $_____
      at the end of the _____ year.
   d. The business will earn a pretax (profit/loss) of $_____ at
      the end of the _____ year.

Business Description

1. Description of the franchise business, from section 1(d) of the
   franchisor's Uniform Franchise Offering Circular:

   _____
   _____
   _____
   _____
   _____
   _____
   _____
   _____
   _____

2. According to the UFOC, in what type of business will the proposed outlet(s) be engaged?

_____

_____

3. What is current primary business address of the owner?

_____

4. Briefly describe the product or service:

_____

_____

5. What is the average or typical price? $_____

6. Besides the owner, how many employees will be required to operate the outlet?
   a. Full time: _____
   b. Part time: _____

7. What is the size of an average or typical outlet?_____ sq. ft.

8. In what type of locality will the outlet be located?
   _____ Commercial
   _____ Light industrial
   _____ Heavy industrial
   _____ Retail site
   _____ Strip center or shopping mall
   _____ Residential
   _____ Recreational/resort
   _____ Other: _____

9. What type of customers will the outlet have?
   _____ Individual consumers
   _____ Businesses
   _____ Institutions/schools
   _____ Government agencies
   _____ Professional practices
   _____ Other: _____

10. Name the leading five competitors for the proposed outlet:
   a. _____
   b. _____
   c. _____
   d. _____
   e. _____

Business History

1. What portions of your background or experience qualify you to own and operate the proposed business?

   _____

   _____

   _____

   _____

   _____

2. When did you first become interested or involved in the industry?

   _____

3. What work experience do you possess that will contribute to your success?

   _____

   _____

   _____

4. Briefly describe the history of the industry:

   _____

   _____

   _____

5. State the specific actions and dates that you have already taken to found and develop the business:

   _____

   _____

The Franchisor

1. Description of the franchisor from section 1 of the Uniform Franchise Offering Circular:

2. According to section 20 of the UFOC (information regarding franchisees of the franchisor) how many franchise outlets are currently sold and open? _____

3. According to section 17 of the UFOC, what is the term of the franchise (i.e., the length of the contract)? _____ years

4. Referring to section 11 of the UFOC, briefly describe the franchisor's training program for franchisees:

_____

_____

_____

Product Description

1. List the proposed outlet's product/service mix by category:
   a. _____
   b. _____
   c. _____
   d. _____
   e. _____

2. List the average or typical price for each product/service category in item 1 above:

	High	Medium	Low
a.	$_____	$_____	$_____
b.	$_____	$_____	$_____
c.	$_____	$_____	$_____
d.	$_____	$_____	$_____
e.	$_____	$_____	$_____

3. Describe any special features, characteristics, patents, etc. that are associated with the products or services:

_____

_____

_____

_____

_____

MARKETING PLAN

Product Analysis

1. Estimate the percentage of total sales that will be derived from:
   ____ Primary products:

   a. _____ _____%

   b. _____ _____%

   c. _____ _____%

   ____ Peripheral products:

   a. _____ _____%

   b. _____ _____%

   c. _____ _____%

   ____ Accessories:

   a. _____ _____%

   b. _____ _____%

   c. _____ _____%

   ____ Supplies:

   a. _____ _____%

   b. _____ _____%

   c. _____ _____%
   ____ Warranty/repair service _____%
   ____ Customer education or training _____%

Customer Analysis

1. Estimate the percentage of total sales that will be derived from each of the following primary customer groups:
   ____ Consumers ____%
   ____ Businesses ____%
   ____ Institutions ____%

2. Identify your product's vertical markets from the following list:
   ____ Accounting/bookkeeping
   ____ Advertising and public relations
   ____ Agribusinesses
   ____ Banking
   ____ Business services
   ____ Construction

____ Counseling
____ Distribution/wholesaling
____ Electronics
____ Engineering
____ Finance
____ Food service
____ Hospitality and lodging
____ Home improvement
____ Industrial engineering
____ Industrial training
____ Interior design
____ Investment planning
____ Law practice
____ Manufacturing
____ Medical/dental practice
____ Personal services
____ Printing/publishing
____ Real estate
____ Retailing

3. Estimate the percentage of total sales that will be derived from the following institutional markets:
____ Education
____ Government administration
____ Health care
____ Military services

Customer Analysis

1. Geographic Analysis
From what geographic areas will the business's customers be derived? Estimate the percentage of total sales that will be derived from each area.
____ City-wide (specify sections or districts, e.g., north city)

_____ _____%
_____ _____%
_____ _____%
_____ _____%
_____ _____%

____ County-wide (specify sections, e.g., north county, or cities)

_____ _____%
_____ _____%

_____ _____%
_____ _____%
_____ _____%
____ State-wide (specify counties, sections, e.g., northern, or cities)
_____ _____%
_____ _____%
_____ _____%
_____ _____%
_____ _____%
____ Nation-wide (specify regions, e.g., northeast)
_____ _____%
_____ _____%
_____ _____%
_____ _____%
_____ _____%
____ World-wide (specify countries)
_____ _____%
_____ _____%
_____ _____%
_____ _____%
_____ _____%

2. Demographic analysis
   What are the characteristics of the business's typical customers? Estimate the percentage of customers who have each characteristic.

   Gender
   Male   _____%
   Female   _____%

   Age
   1–16   _____%
   17–20   _____%
   21–30   _____%
   31–40   _____%
   41–55   _____%

56–65	_____%
65 and over	_____%

Income

Under $10,000	_____%
$10,001–$20,000	_____%
$20,001–$35,000	_____%
$35,001–$50,000	_____%
$50,001–$75,000	_____%
$75,000 and over	_____%

Marital Status

Married	_____%
Divorced	_____%
Single	_____%

Occupation (Specify)

Homemaker	_____%
Office worker	_____%
Executive	_____%
Blue collar worker	_____%
Professional (medical, legal, etc.)	_____%
Agribusiness	_____%
Student	_____%
_____	_____%
_____	_____%
_____	_____%

Sources Consulted prior to the Purchase

Books/magazines	_____%
Salesperson	_____%
Trade show/exhibiton	_____%
Friend or co-worker	_____%
Television/radio	_____%
_____	_____%
_____	_____%
_____	_____%

Factors Influencing the Purchasing Decision

Price	_____%
Quality	_____%
Brand recognition or loyalty	_____%
_____	_____%

_____ _____%
_____ _____%

Other Products/Services Purchased (Specify)
_____ _____%
_____ _____%
_____ _____%
_____ _____%
_____ _____%
_____ _____%
_____ _____%

Hobbies/Interests (Specify)
_____ _____%
_____ _____%
_____ _____%
_____ _____%
_____ _____%

If the franchise outlet will sell to business customers, who are the people who will make the final decision to purchase your product?

_____ Owner/manager
_____ Department or division head
_____ Purchasing agent
_____ Personnel manager
_____ Advertising manager
_____ Secretary
_____ Director (club or association)
_____ Travel agent

_____ _____
_____ _____
_____ _____
_____ _____
_____ _____

Competition Analysis

Copy this worksheet and complete the information below for each of your three major competitors.

Competitor's Business Name: _____

Owner/Manager: _____

Street: _____

City: _____ State: _____ Zip: _____

Telephone: (_____) _____

Year Founded: _____ Territory or market area: _____

Product/Service Mix:

1. _____

2. _____

3. _____

Representative Pricing:

_____ $_____   _____ $_____

_____ $_____   _____ $_____

_____ $_____   _____ $_____

_____ $_____   _____ $_____

_____ $_____   _____ $_____

Estimated Market Share: _____%

Advertising Media Used:

____ Television

    Frequency: _____ Spots per week

    Station(s): _____

    Typical time slots:

    ____ Daytime

    ____ Prime Time

    ____ Late Night

    ____ Newscasts/News Updates

    ____ Movies

____ Radio

    Frequency: _____ Spots per week

    Station(s): _____

    Typical time slots:

    ____ Morning Drive

    ____ Morning to Afternoon

    ____ Evening Drive

_____ Evening to Midnight
_____ Late Night to A.M.
_____ Newscasts
_____ Sports events
_____ Newspaper
Frequency: _____ Times per week
Typical ad size: _____ × _____
_____ Magazine:
Name(s): _____
Frequency: _____ Times per year
Typical ad size: _____ × _____
Advertising Slogans or Themes:

_____
_____
_____
_____

Media Analysis

What media will you use to promote the outlet and advertise its products?

_____ Print
    _____ Metropolitan newspaper: _____
    _____ Suburban newspaper: _____
    _____ General interest magazines:

    _____
    _____
    _____

    _____ Trade publications:

    _____
    _____
    _____

_____ Electronic
    _____ Television stations: _____
    _____ Radio stations: _____
_____ Direct mail
_____ Billboard
_____ Other: _____

Advertising Budget

1. Estimated Quarterly Sales
   January through March   _____% of Annual Sales
   April through June   _____% of Annual Sales
   July through September   _____% of Annual Sales
   October through December _____% of Annual Sales

2. Quarterly Advertising Budget
   Year One   *Annual Sales   Ad Budget*

   January through March   _____% × $_____ = $_____

   April through June   _____% × $_____ = $_____

   July through September   _____% × $_____ = $_____

   October through December _____% × $_____ = $_____

   Year Two   *Annual Sales   Ad Budget*

   January through March   _____% × $_____ = $_____

   April through June   _____% × $_____ = $_____

   July through September   _____% × $_____ = $_____

   October through December _____% × $_____ = $_____

   Year Three   *Annual Sales   Ad Budget*

   January through March   _____% × $_____ = $_____

   April through June   _____% × $_____ = $_____

   July through September   _____% × $_____ = $_____

   October through December _____% × $_____ = $_____

Advertising Plan

Quarter	1 Jan-Mar	2 Apr-Jun	3 Jul-Sep	4 Oct-Dec
Print				
_____	$_____	$_____	$_____	$_____
_____	$_____	$_____	$_____	$_____
TV				
_____	$_____	$_____	$_____	$_____
_____	$_____	$_____	$_____	$_____
Radio				
_____	$_____	$_____	$_____	$_____
_____	$_____	$_____	$_____	$_____
Direct Mail				
_____	$_____	$_____	$_____	$_____
_____	$_____	$_____	$_____	$_____
Totals				
_____	$_____	$_____	$_____	$_____

FINANCIAL PLAN

Projected Sales

1. Estimate the average low, medium, and high price of your outlet's products.

   Low $_____

   Medium $_____

   High $_____

2. Indicate the number of products in each price category that will be sold each month.

   Year 1

	Month					
	1	2	3	4	5	6
Low	_____	_____	_____	_____	_____	_____
Medium	_____	_____	_____	_____	_____	_____
High	_____	_____	_____	_____	_____	_____

	Month					
	7	8	9	10	11	12
Low	_____	_____	_____	_____	_____	_____
Medium	_____	_____	_____	_____	_____	_____
High	_____	_____	_____	_____	_____	_____

   Year 2

	Month					
	1	2	3	4	5	6
Low	_____	_____	_____	_____	_____	_____
Medium	_____	_____	_____	_____	_____	_____
High	_____	_____	_____	_____	_____	_____

	Month					
	7	8	9	10	11	12
Low	_____	_____	_____	_____	_____	_____
Medium	_____	_____	_____	_____	_____	_____
High	_____	_____	_____	_____	_____	_____

Year 3

	Month					
	1	2	3	4	5	6
Low	_____	_____	_____	_____	_____	_____
Medium	_____	_____	_____	_____	_____	_____
High	_____	_____	_____	_____	_____	_____

	Month					
	7	8	9	10	11	12
Low	_____	_____	_____	_____	_____	_____
Medium	_____	_____	_____	_____	_____	_____
High	_____	_____	_____	_____	_____	_____

Proforma Operating Statement

Year 1

	Month					
	1	2	3	4	5	6
Revenues						
Gross Sales	___	___	___	___	___	___
Cost of Goods	___	___	___	___	___	___
Net Revenues	___	___	___	___	___	___
Expenses						
Wages/Salaries	___	___	___	___	___	___
Taxes/Benefits	___	___	___	___	___	___
Commissions	___	___	___	___	___	___
Lease	___	___	___	___	___	___
Utilities	___	___	___	___	___	___
Telephone	___	___	___	___	___	___
Insurance	___	___	___	___	___	___
Supplies	___	___	___	___	___	___
Travel	___	___	___	___	___	___
Maintenance	___	___	___	___	___	___
___	___	___	___	___	___	___
___	___	___	___	___	___	___
___	___	___	___	___	___	___
Total Expenses	___	___	___	___	___	___
Profit/Loss	___	___	___	___	___	___

Year 1

	Month					
	7	8	9	10	11	12
Revenues						
Gross Sales						
Cost of Goods						
Net Revenues						
Expenses						
Wages/Salaries						
Taxes/Benefits						
Commissions						
Lease						
Utilities						
Telephone						
Insurance						
Supplies						
Travel						
Maintenance						
Total Expenses						
Profit/Loss						

Year 2

	Month					
	1	2	3	4	5	6
Revenues						
Gross Sales	____	____	____	____	____	____
Cost of Goods	____	____	____	____	____	____
Net Revenues	____	____	____	____	____	____
Expenses						
Wages/Salaries	____	____	____	____	____	____
Taxes/Benefits	____	____	____	____	____	____
Commissions	____	____	____	____	____	____
Lease	____	____	____	____	____	____
Utilities	____	____	____	____	____	____
Telephone	____	____	____	____	____	____
Insurance	____	____	____	____	____	____
Supplies	____	____	____	____	____	____
Travel	____	____	____	____	____	____
Maintenance	____	____	____	____	____	____
____	____	____	____	____	____	____
____	____	____	____	____	____	____
____	____	____	____	____	____	____
Total Expenses	____	____	____	____	____	____
Profit/Loss	____	____	____	____	____	____

Year 2

			Month			
	7	8	9	10	11	12
Revenues						
Gross Sales	____	____	____	____	____	____
Cost of Goods	____	____	____	____	____	____
Net Revenues	____	____	____	____	____	____
Expenses						
Wages/Salaries	____	____	____	____	____	____
Taxes/Benefits	____	____	____	____	____	____
Commissions	____	____	____	____	____	____
Lease	____	____	____	____	____	____
Utilities	____	____	____	____	____	____
Telephone	____	____	____	____	____	____
Insurance	____	____	____	____	____	____
Supplies	____	____	____	____	____	____
Travel	____	____	____	____	____	____
Maintenance	____	____	____	____	____	____
_____	____	____	____	____	____	____
_____	____	____	____	____	____	____
_____	____	____	____	____	____	____
Total Expenses	____	____	____	____	____	____
Profit/Loss	____	____	____	____	____	____

Year 3

	Month					
	1	2	3	4	5	6
Revenues						
Gross Sales	_____	_____	_____	_____	_____	_____
Cost of Goods	_____	_____	_____	_____	_____	_____
Net Revenues	_____	_____	_____	_____	_____	_____
Expenses						
Wages/Salaries	_____	_____	_____	_____	_____	_____
Taxes/Benefits	_____	_____	_____	_____	_____	_____
Commissions	_____	_____	_____	_____	_____	_____
Lease	_____	_____	_____	_____	_____	_____
Utilities	_____	_____	_____	_____	_____	_____
Telephone	_____	_____	_____	_____	_____	_____
Insurance	_____	_____	_____	_____	_____	_____
Supplies	_____	_____	_____	_____	_____	_____
Travel	_____	_____	_____	_____	_____	_____
Maintenance	_____	_____	_____	_____	_____	_____
_____	_____	_____	_____	_____	_____	_____
_____	_____	_____	_____	_____	_____	_____
_____	_____	_____	_____	_____	_____	_____
Total Expenses	_____	_____	_____	_____	_____	_____
Profit/Loss	_____	_____	_____	_____	_____	_____

Year 3

	Month					
	7	8	9	10	11	12
Revenues						
Gross Sales	___	___	___	___	___	___
Cost of Goods	___	___	___	___	___	___
Net Revenues	___	___	___	___	___	___
Expenses						
Wages/Salaries	___	___	___	___	___	___
Taxes/Benefits	___	___	___	___	___	___
Commissions	___	___	___	___	___	___
Lease	___	___	___	___	___	___
Utilities	___	___	___	___	___	___
Telephone	___	___	___	___	___	___
Insurance	___	___	___	___	___	___
Supplies	___	___	___	___	___	___
Travel	___	___	___	___	___	___
Maintenance	___	___	___	___	___	___
___	___	___	___	___	___	___
___	___	___	___	___	___	___
___	___	___	___	___	___	___
Total Expenses	___	___	___	___	___	___
Profit/Loss	___	___	___	___	___	___

PROFORMA FINANCIAL STATEMENT

Assets

   Current Assets

      Cash on hand

      Accounts receivable   _____

      Inventory   _____

      Prepaid expenses   _____

      _____   _____

      _____   _____

   Total Current Assets   _____

   Fixed Assets

      Real estate   _____

      Vehicles/equipment   _____

      Furnishings/fixtures   _____

      _____   _____

      _____   _____

   Total Fixed Assets   _____

   Total Assets   _____

Liabilities & Owner's Equity

   Current Liabilities

      Taxes payable   _____

      Debt service   _____

      _____   _____

      _____   _____

   Total Current Liabilities   _____

   Long-Term Debt   _____

   Total Liabilities   _____

   Owner's Equity   _____

   Total Liabilities & Owner's Equity   _____

Index